Costing and C⸺ for Catering

Janet Hughes and Brian Ireland

Stanley Thornes (Publishers) Ltd

Other books in Catering and Food Science from ST(P):

The Prevention of Food Poisoning by Jill Trickett

An Introduction to Hotel and Catering Economics by Chris Ryan

Food Hygiene – A Study Guide by P. A. Alcock

Text: © J Hughes & B Ireland 1981
Illustrations: © Stanley Thornes (Publishers) Ltd 1981

First published in 1981 by:
Stanley Thornes (Publishers) Ltd
Educa House
Old Station Drive
Leckhampton
CHELTENHAM GL53 0DN

Reprinted 1988

British Library Cataloguing in Publication Data

Hughes, Janet
    Costing and calculations for catering.
    1. Food service — Mathematics
    2. Food service — Cost control
    I. Title   II. Ireland, Brian
    510'.2'4642   TXC911.3.M/

    ISBN 0-85950-493-X

Typeset by Permanent Typesetting & Printing Co., Ltd.
Printed and bound in Great Britain at The Bath Press, Avon.

Contents

Preface

The object of this book is to combine a number of areas of general interest to the caterer and student alike in one volume. It is hoped that it has been written and presented in such a way as to remove some, if not all, of the mystery behind many of the problems that arise within the catering industry.

Many of the examples given or facts stated have been drawn from the practical experience of the authors, who have tried to provide the answers to many of the problems they have been faced with over the last fifteen years or so of managing and operating hotels and other catering establishments.

A number of statements appear throughout the book with which, it is hoped, the reader will take issue. Part of the idea of the book is to stimulate thought and discussion and, with luck, the reader with a friend or lecturer, will be able to expand some of the ideas set out.

From an academic point of view, the book is aimed to provide the basic study matter for students embarking on City and Guilds Courses 705 and 706; OND/TEC first year; and the HND/TEC Higher Diploma first year; and HCIMA, Part 1.

Finally, the authors would like to wish all students and prospective caterers every good fortune in their careers, and sincerely hope that they will be able to improve the present standards of catering and their profitability in the United Kingdom out of all recognition!

JANET HUGHES
BRIAN IRELAND

Notes on the Authors

Janet Hughes FHCIMA BEd

Past lecturer in applied catering studies at many Colleges of Further Education and Technology including: Birmingham, Bournemouth and Stratford upon Avon, to students following courses for professional qualifications in the Hotel and Catering Industry. A past examiner for City & Guilds and HCIMA, and assessor for the Joint Committee awarding National Diplomas in Catering & Hotel Operations. Holder of senior appointments in residential and educational establishments and a variety of positions in many branches of the catering industry.

Brian Ireland FHCIMA

Currently a Senior Lecturer in Hotel and Catering Management at The South Warwickshire College of Further Education in Stratford upon Avon. Formerly a hotel manager and restaurateur, an examiner in Book-keeping for the Royal Society of Arts, and an examiner in Book-keeping and Food Costing for the U.E.I. Also manages a business consultancy operation specialising in business systems, computer operations, stock control and feasability.

1
Arithmetical Operations

Introduction

Before you can attempt calculations in catering you must be able to manage the basic operations of arithmetic: *adding, subtracting, multiplying* and *dividing*. You need to know how to work with *fractions*, *decimals* and *percentages* too. This chapter gives a number of exercises, and you need to be able to understand these and complete them accurately before you can tackle the more difficult problems of 'real life' later in the book.

Basic definitions

Here are some definitions which should be learnt and understood.

(i)   When two or more numbers are added together the result is called the *sum*.

(ii) When one number is taken from another (or subtracted) the result is called the *difference*.

(iii) When numbers are multiplied together the result is known as the *product*.

(iv) If numbers are to be divided or shared out, the numbers are given a special name according to their function in the operation. Consider e.g.
$$108 \div 4 = 27$$
The number being divided into (108) is the *dividend*, the number doing the dividing (4) is the *divisor*, the result (27) is the *quotient*.

EXERCISE 1

1. The sum of 28 and 10 is ___38___ .

2. The product of 7 and 9 is ___54___ .

3. The difference between 21 and 1 is ___20___ .

4. The quotient of $115 \div 5$ is ___23___ .

5. The dividend in 1762 ÷ 12 is __146,.8__

6. The divisor in 2096 ÷ 8 is __262__.

Addition

When two or more numbers are added together an addition sum is completed. In catering there is often a need to add columns of figures up, down and horizontally. In this case the rules should be:

(i) First add up, then down.

(ii) Then add from right to left and check back from left to right. The bottom right-hand column total column should be the same for all the total columns.

Example

A restaurant has three till waitresses and their checks for the meal period were as follows:

Waitress	1	2	3	Total
	£ p	£ p	£ p	£ p
	2.73	2.78	2.75	8.26
	2.66	2.69	2.69	8.04
	2.79	2.68	2.68	8.15
	2.67	2.60	2.73	8.00
	2.78	2.79	2.79	8.36
	13.63	13.54	13.64	40.81

The figure £40.81 will give the total sales for the meal period. The check totals will be obtained by registering what the customer has bought and its price and then totalling up the cost.

EXERCISE 2

Add to complete the following tables:

1. £ p	£ p	£ p	£ p	£ p	£ p	£ p
26.32	280.46	926.33	24.52	167.84	4913.81	
41.22	32.87	41.26	145.11	222.45	231.90	
113.56	22.64	11.83	29.00	12.68	1247.13	
33.23	334.19	112.76	431.98	1379.22	12.68	
214,33	670,16	1092,18	630,61	1783,19	6405,52	

2.

£ p	£ p	£ p	£ p	£ p	£ p
15.31	15.56	15.91	16.42	17.10	
16.65	16.93	17.30	17.86	18.60	
16.97	17.07	17.25	17.91	18.65	
18.34	18.44	18.64	19.35	20.15	
20.25	20.48	20.81	21.60	22.50	
21.60	21.84	22.20	23.04	24.00	

3.

£ p	£ p	£ p	£ p	£ p	£ p
19.81	20.03	20.59	21.36	22.25	
20.65	21.00	21.22	22.03	22.94	
20.65	21.00	21.22	22.03	22.94	
22.00	22.37	22.61	23.46	24.44	
20.50	20.50	20.50	20.50	20.50	
21.00	21.00	21.00	21.00	21.00	
24.00	24.00	24.00	24.00	24.00	
25.00	25.00	25.00	25.00	25.00	
35.00	35.00	35.00	35.00	35.00	

4.

£ p	£ p	£ p	£ p	£ p	£ p
26.26	26.55	27.29	28.32	29.50	
39.40	39.40	39.40	39.40	39.40	
44.75	44.75	44.75	44.75	44.75	
21.00	21.00	21.00	21.00	21.00	
22.50	22.50	22.50	22.50	22.50	
31.00	31.00	31.00	31.00	31.00	
32.00	32.00	32.00	32.00	32.00	
35.00	35.00	35.00	35.00	35.00	
49.00	49.00	49.00	49.00	49.00	
39.00	39.00	39.00	39.00	39.00	
27.50	27.50	27.50	27.50	27.50	
28.00	28.00	28.00	28.00	28.00	
37.75	37.75	37.75	37.75	37.75	

Subtraction

When a small amount is taken from a larger amount, e.g. when you are giving change or finding out the amount of stock used from the shelves, it is always possible to check that the answer is correct by adding the difference to the smaller number.

Examples

(1) Amount of money offered   10.00 −
      Cost of cheque   3.97
                          £ 6.03 change required

                         £ p
     To check: 3.97 +
                     6.03
                  10.00

(2)

Commodity	Column 1 Stock in hand	Column 2 Stock left	Column 3 Stock used
A.10 can peaches	20	8	12
A.10 can pineapple	13	5	8
A.10 can apricots	5	0	5

If Columns 2 and 3 are added, the sum should equal Column 1.

EXERCISE 3

Subtract:

1. £ p	2. £ p	3. £ p	4. £ p	5. £ p	6. £ p
15.79	124.87	2453.76	2224.51	4251.92	1654.96
2.98	64.16	2369.81	1598.70	4092.35	942.99

Multiplication

This is really 'quick addition'. 5 × 6 is, in fact, the same as 5 + 5 + 5 + 5 + 5 + 5. The answers in single digit multiplication are best learnt, though multiplication squares can be used. When two digits or more are used in the number to be multiplied, the operation is known as *long multiplication* and may be done by one of the following methods:

Method 1
278 × 317

The figures are set down under each other:

    278 ×
    317

The key to multiplying is to start each line of working under the figure you are multiplying.

i.e.　when multiplying by 7, start the line of working under 7
　　　when multiplying by 1, start the line of working under 1
　　　when multiplying by 3, start the line of working under 3.

Carry out the three lines of working:

```
    278
    317
  1 946
  2 78
 83 4
 88 126
```

Fill the gaps with a nought if this helps addition. At all times the units must be kept under each other.

```
    278
    317
  1 946
  2 780
 83 400
 88 126
```

The same rules apply if the multiplying is started at the left-hand side of figure instead of the right:

```
278 ×
317
```

i.e.　when multiplying by 3, start each line of working under 3
　　　when multiplying by 1, start each line of working under 1
　　　when multiplying by 7, start each line of working under 7.

Method 2

```
    278      or        278
    317                317
   83 4              83 400
   2 78              2 780
  1 946             1 946
 88 126            88 126
```

COSTING AND CALCULATIONS FOR CATERING

Remember: if multiplying by the power of 10, add the same number of 0 as in the multiplier:

Examples

$$\text{(1)} \quad 65 \times \overset{(1)}{1}0 = 650 \quad (+1)$$

$$\text{(3)} \quad 678 \times 1000 = 678\,000 \quad (+3)$$

$$\text{(2)} \quad 287 \times \overset{(2)}{1}00 = 28\,700 \quad (+2)$$

For quickness, if multiplying by a multiplier near a power of 10, e.g. 99, 101, 999, multiply by the power of 10 then add or subtract the multiplicand as required:

$$653 \times 99 = 65\,300 - 653 = 65\,953$$
$$719 \times 101 = 71\,900 + 719 = 72\,619$$

The multiplicand is the original number to be multiplied. In the above examples the multiplicands are:

(1) 65,
(2) 284,
(3) 678.

EXERCISE 4

1. Multiply the following:
   (a) $6\,039 \times 1\,204$ (b) $9\,548 \times 1\,125$ (c) $2\,437 \times 1\,809$ (d) $2\,371 \times 155$

2. Multiply the following using the 'quick method':
   (a) 977×102 (b) 477×99 (c) 688×99.9

Division

When the divisor is a number for which you know the multiplication tables short division is worked.

Example
Divide 17 236 by 9.

$$9)\overline{17\,235}$$
$$1\,915$$

Often it helps if you know a number can be divided by a given number without having to work the division.

The following could be advantageously learnt:

A number is divisible by:

    2   if the right-hand digit is even

    3   if the sum of the digits is divisible by 3

    4   if the number composed of the last two digits is divisible by 4

    5   if the right-hand digit is 5 or 0

    6   if the number is divisible by both 2 and 3

    8   if the number composed of the last 3 digits is divisible by 8

    9   if the sum of the digits is divisible by 9

  10   if the number ends in 0

  11   if the sum of 1st, 3rd, 5th etc. digits and the sum of the 2nd, 4th, 6th etc. digits is divisible by 11 or is 0

  12   if the number is divisible by 3 or 4.

Other helpful short cuts:

(i)   To divide by power of 10 put a point at the end of the right-hand figure and move it to the left for each 0 in the divisor.

Example

    $38 \div 10 = 3.8$ $3789 \div 100 = 37.89$ $197 \div 1000 = 0.197$

(ii)   To divide by 5, first multiply by 2 then divide by 10.

(iii) To divide by 25, first multiply by 4 then divide by 100.

Long division

This method has to be used when the divisor is a number for which you do not know your tables and is set out in the following way:

Examples

(1)   Divide 7632 by 53.

$$\begin{array}{r} 1 \\ 53\overline{)7632} \end{array}$$

Then say: 53 into 7 will not go.

            53 into 76 will go how many times? 1, so the 1 is put as part of the quotient over the last figure we are considering, i.e. 6.

Then multiply 53 by 1 and write the product under the figures 76. These two figures must then be subtracted:

$$\begin{array}{r} 1 \\ 53\overline{)7632} \\ 53 \\ \hline 23 \end{array}$$

        53 will not go into 23 so 'bring down' the 3:

```
        14
    53)7632
        53
       233
```

53 into 233 will go how many times? 4, so put the 4 into the quotient over the 1st figure brought down.

The sum is continued in the same way until the sum is complete:

```
       144
    53)7632
       53
      233
      212
      212
```

If there is a remainder, it may be put over the divisor and left as a fraction or worked on by putting a point after the right-hand digit of the dividend and adding 0, continuing the division to give 2 or 3 decimal places (see page 10).

(2)   Divide 2647 by 523.

Either

```
           5
    523)2647
        2615
         32 remainder
```

Quotient: $5\dfrac{32}{523}$

or

```
         5.0612
    523)2647
        2615
        3200
        3138
         620
         523
        1070
        1046
          24 remainder
```

Quotient: 5.061 to 3 decimal places

EXERCISE 5

1. Divide by short division and apply divisibility tests or short cuts:

    (a) 45 ÷ 5   (b) 75 ÷ 3   (c) 121 ÷ 11   (d) 158 ÷ 12   (e) 224 ÷ 8

2. Divide correct to 2 decimal places:

    (a) 718374 ÷ 782   (b) 85702 ÷ 128
    (c) 7953.6 ÷ 25.3   (d) 1293078 ÷ 2036
    (e) 16.843 ÷ 2.2   (f) 54.709 ÷ 25
    (g) 431 ÷ 52   (h) 1086 ÷ 13
    (i) 5000 ÷ 23.3   (j) 2377 ÷ 0.005

3. Divide, correct to two decimal places (if in any doubt, see page 10):

    (a) 476 by 12   (b) 6742 by 14   (c) 68472 by 24
    (d) 67468 by 278   (e) 456 by 413   (f) 698947 by 3764
    (g) 14 by 16   (h) 234 by 244   (i) 400 by 600
    (j) 674 by 898

Decimals

Any digit takes on a different value according to the position it occupies in any particular number. Our number system is a *denary* system, i.e. it uses units of 10 and *decimals*.

In the number 777 the same digit 7 has three different values according to its place:

    H   T   U
    7   7   7

The right-hand digit = 7 Units

The middle digit   = 7 Tens

The left-hand digit = 7 Hundreds

Each 'place value' thus increased by a factor 10 as we move from right to left and each place value decreases by a factor of 10 as we move from left to right, to become tenths, hundredths, thousandths.

We could have a number:

Th	H	T	U	Tenths	Hundredths	Thousandths
1000	100	10	1	1/10	1/100	1/1000
5	0	6	2	5	8	3

This indicates:

$(5 \times 1000) + (0 \times 100) + (6 \times 10) + (2 \times 1) + (5 \times 1/10) + (8 \times 1/100) + (3 \times 1/1000)$

This is rather cumbersome, to say the least, so a neater form is available that separates the integral part (whole number) from the decimal part by a dot or decimal point, i.e.

$$\underbrace{5062}_{} \cdot \underbrace{583}_{}$$

integral part͞ ͞ ͞ ͞ decimal part

The decimal part represents $\dfrac{583}{1000}$ which is clearly a fraction and so .583 is called a *decimal fraction*.

Note that when a decimal fraction .321 has no integral part, you should get into the habit of putting a zero to the left of the decimal point, i.e. .321 should be written 0.321. This will avoid problems. Note also that the way to say 38.372 is 'thirty eight point three seven two'. Similarly, 0.321 is read as 'nought point three two one'. If a number has both an integral part and a decimal part it is referred to as a *mixed number*.

Decimal places and significant figures

The number of figures to the right of the decimal point indicates the number of decimal places that the number contains. For example:

    6.72   has 2 decimal places
    0.0075 has 4 decimal places
    12.5   has 1 decimal place

All the figures to the right of the decimal point count, including zeros.

All figures that affect the value of a decimal number are called *significant figures* and include digits to the left of the point as well as the right. For example:

    87326   has 5 significant figures
        2.54 has 3 significant figures

Initial and final zeros do not normally count as significant figures. For example:

    0.000763 has 3 significant figures
    0.003   has 1 significant figure

Zeros between digits, however, *are* significant. For example:

    0.06040   has 3 significant figures

Example
How many decimal places and significant figures are there in 29.6, 105.37, 0.046, 13800, 0.00042, 12.360 and 0.0604?

	Decimal Places	Significant figures
29.6	1	3
105.37	2	5
0.046	3	2
13800	0	3
0.00042	5	2
12.360	3	4
0.0604	4	3

EXERCISE 6

In each of the following state: (a) the number of decimal places; (b) the number of significant figures.

1. 71.301   **2.** 1000.01   **3.** 5427   **4.** 20.045

5. 0.0356   **6.** 7.050   **7.** 18.003   **8.** 240

Addition and subtraction of decimals

The most important thing to remember when adding and subtracting numbers with decimal points in is to arrange the numbers so that the decimal point is always directly underneath the preceding one.

Examples
(1) 3.647 + 23.56 + 0.402 + 407.5 should be written as follows:

$$
\begin{array}{r}
2.647 + \\
23.56 \\
0.402 \\
407.5 \\
\hline
435.109 \\
\hline
\end{array}
$$

The columns must be neatly aligned.

(2) 16.28 − 9.032 should be written as:

$$
\begin{array}{r}
16.28 \\
- \quad 9.032 \\
\hline
7.248 \\
\hline
\end{array}
$$

EXERCISE 7

1. Add:
  (a) 4.321 + 16.56 + 2.416 + 34.201   (b) 12.206 + 4.73 + 5.78 + 20.88
  (c) 463.7 + 28.4 + 31.52 + 34.86

2. Subtract:

(a) 50.7 − 23.2
(b) 12.164 − 3.026
(c) 105.28 − 93.076

Multiplication of decimals

It is generally easier when multiplying decimals to ignore the point during the arithmetical calculation and put it into the product at the end.

Examples

(1) Evaluate 38.74 × 0.614.

38.74   2 decimal places
0.614   3 decimal places

Ignore the point and work out as on page 5:

```
    3874
     614
   14496
   38740
 2324400
 2377636
```

Now count up the numbers of decimal places 2 + 3 = 5 decimal places. Put the point after the last digit in the number i.e. after 6 and move it 5 places to the left.

i.e. 23.7.7.6.3.6.   *Answer* = 23.77636
    5 4 3 2 1

To make sure the point is in the correct place, carry out a rough check as follows:

40 × 0.6 = 24

This proves that the point is in the right place.

(2) Evaluate 125.05 × 0.99.

125.05 ×   2 places
0.99   2 places

```
   12505
      99
  112545
 1125450
 1237995
```
Move the decimal point 4 places.

Answer = 123.7995

Rough check:

   125 × 1 = 125

So the point is in the right place.

EXERCISE 8

Evaluate the following by long division, giving the answers to the significant figures or decimal places required. Apply a rough check to verify the answers.

1. 86.51 × 8.63, to 3 decimal places.   **2.** 32.37 × 32.7, to 7 significant figures.

3. 4.012 × 344, to 2 decimal places.

Division of decimals

When dividing remember:

   dividend ÷ divisor = quotient

or

   $\dfrac{\text{dividend}}{\text{divisor}}$ = quotient

Also, revise the rules for long division (see pages 7-8).

Example
Divide 28.376 by 5.6.

This could be written as $\dfrac{28.376}{5.6}$

To divide it is necessary to make the divisor a whole number. This can be done by multiplying it by 10, i.e. by moving the point 1 place to the right: 56. Later on when studying fractions you will discover that you can multiply or divide the top and bottom of a fraction by the same number without altering its value, so 28.376 ÷ 5.6 must become 283.76 ÷ 56. Set this out as a long division. Always put the point in the quotient above the point in the dividend:

```
       5.067
   56)283.76
      280
        3 76
        3 36
         400
```

Answer = 5.07 correct to 2 decimal places.

Rough check $28 \div 5 = 5\frac{3}{5} = 5.6$. Therefore the answer is correct.

When correcting decimal places to the nearest stated number, always work to one place more and correct it 'up' or 'down' according to the following rules. When the last digit is 4 or below, do not change the last but one digit, if last digit is 5 or more, increase the last but one digit by 1. Always remove the last figure after correction when writing out the answer.

Examples

(1)   287.362 to 2 decimal places
          = 287.36

(2)   397.4689 to 3 decimal places
          = 397.469

For the division of decimals, learn the following rules:

(i)   Always convert the divisor to a whole number by moving the decimal point the required number to the right.

(ii)   Move the decimal point in the dividend the same number of places to the right.

(iii)   Set out as a long division sum and put the decimal point in the quotient directly above the decimal point in the dividend.

Example
Evaluate $77.372 \div 11.02$ to 2 decimal places.

```
              7.021
      1102)7737.2
           7714
            23 20
            22 04
             1 160
             1 102
                58
```

Answer = 7.02 correct to 2 decimal places.

Rough check: $\frac{77}{11}$ or $11\overline{)77} = 7$, so the decimal point is in the right place.

EXERCISE 9

1.   Evaluate the following to 3 decimal places:
     (a) $745.8 \div 11.5$ (b) $8.058 \div 2.37$ (c) $5932 \div 4.6$

2.   Evaluate the following to 3 significant figures:
     (a) $885.5 \div 3.22$ (b) $1728 \div 0.012$ (c) $5932 \div 0.46$

Fractions

If a Gâteau is divided into 12 equal parts and a waitress serves 5 portions to one table, she could be said to have served five twelfths or $\frac{5}{12}$ of the Gâteau to that table. We call $\frac{5}{12}$ a fraction. The number on top (5) is called a *numerator* and the number below (12) a *denominator*. We can always say that a fraction $= \frac{\text{numerator}}{\text{denominator}}$.

When the top number is smaller than the bottom, the fraction is said to be a *proper* or *vulgar* fraction. This means it must be a quantity less than 1.

If the top number is larger than the bottom, it is called a *top-heavy* or *improper fraction*, e.g. $\frac{17}{12}$. A number made up of a whole number and a fraction, such as $2\frac{3}{4}$, is called a *mixed number*. A top-heavy fraction can be changed to a mixed number as shown in the following two examples.

In print, fractions can be written as $2\frac{3}{4}$, $2\frac{3}{4}$, $2\frac{3}{4}$, and these forms are used in this text.

Examples

(1)   Write $\frac{17}{12}$ as a mixed number.

Divide the denominator into the numerator:

$$12\overline{)17} = 1 \text{ remainder } 5$$

This means that when we divide 12 into 17 we have five twelfths or $\frac{5}{12}$ left over. So we can write $\frac{17}{12}$ as $1 + \frac{5}{12}$ or $1\frac{5}{12}$.

(2)   Write $2\frac{3}{7}$ as a top-heavy fraction.

$2\frac{3}{7}$ is $2 + \frac{3}{7}$. How many sevenths are there in 2? Answer: 14 because $2 \times 7 = 14$. How many sevenths in $\frac{3}{7}$? Answer: 3. Therefore there are 17 sevenths altogether and we can write this as $\frac{17}{7}$.

If a fraction is found to be written with the top and bottom the same, it has a value of 1, e.g. $\frac{25}{25} = 1$, $\frac{3}{3} = 1$, $\frac{9}{9} = 1$.

EXERCISE 10

Here are some fractions:

(a) $\dfrac{5}{8}$ (b) $\dfrac{5}{5}$ (c) $\dfrac{9}{17}$ (d) $\dfrac{6}{5}$ (e) $\dfrac{13}{9}$

(f) $2\dfrac{3}{8}$ (g) $\dfrac{21}{4}$ (h) $\dfrac{12}{9}$ (i) $\dfrac{11}{11}$ (j) $\dfrac{4}{2}$

1. State the denominator in (a), (c), (f) and (i).

2. State the numerator in (b), (e), (j) and (h).

3. Which fractions have the value of 1?

4. Which are improper fractions?

5. Which fractions are proper?

6. Which are the mixed number fractions?

7. Which is the whole number in (f)?

8. Change to mixed numbers:

    (a) $\dfrac{28}{9}$ (b) $\dfrac{11}{2}$ (c) $\dfrac{21}{5}$ (d) $\dfrac{38}{13}$ (e) $\dfrac{28}{9}$

9. Change to improper fractions:

    (a) $2\dfrac{1}{5}$ (b) $7\dfrac{3}{12}$ (c) $1\dfrac{3}{8}$ (d) $5\dfrac{11}{15}$ (e) $2\dfrac{3}{18}$

10. Write out 3 vulgar fractions and circle the denominators in each.

Cancelling fractions

When dealing with fractions it is possible to multiply the top and bottom by the same figure without altering its value. For example:

$$\frac{5}{8} = \frac{25}{40} = \frac{30}{48} = \frac{10}{16}$$

Similarly, the top and bottom figures can be divided by the same figure and provided there is no remainder, the value is still the same.

$$\frac{15}{20} = \frac{3}{4} \qquad \frac{20}{30} = \frac{4}{6} = \frac{2}{3}$$

When no further division can be carried out, the fraction is said to be in its *lowest* and *simplest* form. This process of dividing the numerator and denominator by the same number or common factor is known as *cancelling*. When you work out fractions the answer should always be given in its lowest form and if necessary as a mixed number. *Never divide by zero*, as this has no meaning.

EXERCISE 11

Express the following in their lowest or simplest form, using a mixed number in the answer if necessary:

1. $\dfrac{168}{105}$ 2. $\dfrac{45}{150}$ 3. $\dfrac{240}{360}$ 4. $\dfrac{30}{9}$ 5. $\dfrac{36}{16}$

6. $\dfrac{40}{70}$ 7. $\dfrac{9}{27}$ 8. $\dfrac{36}{60}$ 9. $\dfrac{8}{12}$ 10. $\dfrac{55}{60}$

Addition and subtraction of fractions

Before it is possible to add and subtract fractions, they must be put over the same denominator, that is, a number that all the denominators in the sum will divide into.

Example

$$\frac{3}{4} + \frac{2}{5} + \frac{7}{10}.$$

The lowest number which 4, 5 and 10 will all divide into is 20. This is said to be the *lowest common denominator* so that $\frac{3}{4}$, $\frac{2}{5}$ and $\frac{7}{10}$ have all now to be put over 20.

This is done by dividing the denominator in the fraction into the common denominator and multiplying the answer by the numerator:

$$20 \div 4 = 5 \qquad 5 \times 3 = 15$$
$$20 \div 5 = 4 \qquad 4 \times 2 = 8$$
$$20 \div 10 = 2 \qquad 2 \times 7 = 14$$

So $\dfrac{3}{4} + \dfrac{2}{5} + \dfrac{7}{10} = \dfrac{15}{20} + \dfrac{8}{20} + \dfrac{14}{20}$ or $\dfrac{15 + 8 + 14}{20}$

If the numerator is added, this gives $\dfrac{37}{20}$ which can be expressed in its simplest form as a mixed number, $1\dfrac{17}{20}$.

If the sum is made up of mixed numbers, the whole numbers are added first and then the fractions are worked out separately as above.

Example

Add $2\dfrac{1}{5} + 3\dfrac{2}{8} + 1\dfrac{1}{20}$.

Add the whole numbers: $2 + 3 + 1 = 6$.

To add the fractions, find the common denominator, 40

$$40 \div 5 = 8 \qquad 8 \times 1 = 8$$
$$40 \div 8 = 5 \qquad 5 \times 2 = 10$$
$$40 \div 20 = 2 \qquad 2 \times 1 = 2$$

So $\dfrac{1}{5} + \dfrac{2}{8} + \dfrac{1}{20} = \dfrac{8 + 10 + 2}{40} = \dfrac{2\cancel{0}}{4\cancel{0}} = \dfrac{\cancel{2}^{1}}{\cancel{4}_{2}} = \dfrac{1}{2}$

Answer $= 6 + \dfrac{1}{2} = 6\dfrac{1}{2}$.

When subtracting, the same rules apply, but the minus sign is observed.

Examples

(1) $\dfrac{1}{2} - \dfrac{1}{4}$.

The lowest common denominator is 4:

$$4 \div 2 = 2 \qquad 2 \times 1 = 2$$
$$4 \div 4 = 1 \qquad 1 \times 1 = 1$$

So $\dfrac{1}{2} \div \dfrac{1}{4} = \dfrac{2 - 1}{4} = \dfrac{1}{4}$.

(2) $4\dfrac{3}{8} - 3\dfrac{1}{12}$.

Subtract the whole numbers: $4 - 3 = 1$.

The lowest common denominator is 24:
$$24 \div 8 = 3 \qquad 3 \times 3 = 9$$
$$24 \div 12 = 2 \qquad 2 \times 1 = 2$$

So $\dfrac{3}{8} - \dfrac{1}{12} = \dfrac{9 - 2}{24} = \dfrac{7}{24}$

Answer $= 1\dfrac{7}{24}$.

EXERCISE 12

1. $5\dfrac{3}{4} + 1\dfrac{2}{3} - 2\dfrac{5}{5}$
2. $3\dfrac{1}{5} + 1\dfrac{4}{8} - 2\dfrac{9}{20}$

3. $2\dfrac{1}{2} - 1\dfrac{1}{3} + 3\dfrac{1}{4}$
4. $3\dfrac{3}{4} + 5\dfrac{1}{2} - 2\dfrac{1}{4} - 1\dfrac{5}{13}$

5. $\dfrac{1}{8} - \dfrac{1}{12} + \dfrac{2}{3} + \dfrac{5}{7}$

Multiplication of fractions

The simplest way to multiply fractions is to multiply the numerators and multiply the denominators, then cancel them out to their lowest form.

Example

$$\frac{2}{8} \times \frac{1}{3} \times \frac{5}{10} = \frac{2 \times 1 \times 5}{8 \times 3 \times 10} = \frac{10}{240} = \frac{1}{24}$$

In this example the multiplication would be simpler if the cancelling were done first:

$$\frac{\overset{1}{\cancel{2}}}{\underset{4}{\cancel{8}}} \times \frac{1}{3} \times \frac{5}{10} \qquad \text{cancel by 2}$$

$$= \frac{1}{4} \times \frac{1}{3} \times \frac{\overset{1}{\cancel{5}}}{\underset{2}{\cancel{10}}} \qquad \text{cancel by 5}$$

$$= \frac{1}{4} \times \frac{1}{3} \times \frac{1}{2}$$

$$= \frac{1 \times 1 \times 1}{4 \times 3 \times 2}$$

$$= \frac{1}{24}$$

Some examples have mixed numbers, so before multiplication can take place the mixed numbers must be turned into improper fractions and then the method above used.

Example

$$3\frac{3}{5} \times 1\frac{1}{15} \times \frac{5}{20}$$

$$= \frac{18}{\underset{1}{\cancel{5}}} \times \frac{16}{15} \times \frac{\overset{1}{\cancel{5}}}{20} \qquad \text{cancel by 5}$$

$$= \frac{18}{1} \times \frac{\overset{4}{\cancel{16}}}{15} \times \frac{1}{\underset{5}{\cancel{20}}} \qquad \text{cancel by 4}$$

$$= \frac{\overset{6}{\cancel{18}}}{1} \times \frac{4}{\underset{5}{\cancel{15}}} \times \frac{1}{5} \qquad \text{cancel by 3}$$

$$= \frac{6 \times 4 \times 1}{1 \times 5 \times 5}$$

$$= \frac{24}{25}$$

This method of writing out the answer is very time-consuming, and it is possible to do all the cancelling together if figures are kept neat and crossed out clearly.

Example

$$3\frac{3}{7} \times \frac{28}{30} \times 3\frac{1}{3}$$

$$= \frac{24^8}{7_1} \times \frac{28^4}{30_1} \times \frac{10^1}{3} = \frac{8 \times 4 \times 1}{1 \times 1 \times 3}$$

$$= \frac{32}{3}$$

$$= 10\frac{2}{3}$$

EXERCISE 13

1. $1\frac{1}{2} \times 6\frac{3}{8}$ 2. $3\frac{1}{8} \times 2\frac{2}{9}$ 3. $\frac{1}{4}$ of 28   4. $3\frac{1}{9}$ of $108\frac{3}{5}$

5. $\frac{1}{9}$ of 27   6. $\frac{11}{13}$ of 19   7. $27\frac{1}{3} \times 1\frac{1}{4}$ 8. $2\frac{1}{12} \times \frac{1}{15}$

Division of fractions

Once the skill of multiplying fractions has been achieved it is then possible to carry out division of fractions if the following rule is learnt: To divide fractions turn the divisor upside down and multiply. Problem: which is the divisor? It is always the fraction or worked out bracket after the division sign. In Example 1 below, for instance, the divisor is $\frac{5}{9}$.

Examples

(1) $\quad \frac{2}{3} \div \frac{5}{9} = \frac{2}{3_1} \times \frac{9^3}{5} = \frac{6}{5} = 1\frac{1}{5}$

(2) $\quad 1\frac{11}{12} \div \frac{3}{24} \div \frac{8}{15} = \frac{23}{12_1} \times \frac{24^2}{3_1} \times \frac{15^5}{8_4} = \frac{23 \times 1 \times 5}{1 \times 1 \times 4}$

$$= \frac{115}{4} = 28\frac{3}{4}$$

EXERCISE 14

1. $3\frac{4}{7} \div 1\frac{1}{14}$ 2. $6\frac{3}{5} \div 2\frac{3}{4}$ 3. $1\frac{7}{15} \div 2\frac{14}{15}$ 4. $\frac{5}{36} \div \frac{5}{4}$

5. $7\frac{1}{2} \div \frac{3}{5}$ 6. $\frac{18}{25} \div 4\frac{4}{5}$ 7. $12 \div \frac{9}{10}$ 8. $3\frac{3}{4} \div \frac{1}{2}$

Precedence rules

In all the examples given so far only simple arithmetical operations have been considered. Often problems produce a mixture of operations and these must be carried out in a special sequence, i.e. in the right order. Multiplication and division is always done before addition and subtraction. However, a further complication is introduced with brackets, and these must always be worked first and if there are inner and outer brackets work from inside out.

Example

Simplify $198 - [(6 + 12) \times (22 - 16)] + 12$.

Rule. Work out brackets from within out.

Simplify inner bracket: $198 - [18 \times 6] + 12$

Work out outer bracket: $198 - 108 + 12$

Then work from left to right.

Add next: $198 + 12$

              $= 210$

Subtract: 108

to give 102

This can be done in one stage by putting in a bracket:

        $(198 + 12) - 108$

  $= 210 - 108$

  $= 102$

When working fractions and if the word 'of' occurs in the expression note:

(i)   Though it means multiply this is stronger than the sign $\times$ so it worked out first. To help remember the sequence of operations remember

$$
\begin{array}{cccccc}
\text{B} & \text{O} & \text{D} & \text{M} & \text{A} & \text{S} \\
\diagup & | & | & | & | & | \\
\text{Brackets} & \text{of} & \div & \times & + & -
\end{array}
$$

Try to invent a sentence using the initials in sequence, such as

   Brother of Dad Married Aunt Sal!

(ii)   If a fraction line is in the expression this is a form of bracket but indicates that the whole of the numerator must be divided by the whole of the denominator.

Example

$$\frac{3\frac{10}{11} - 1\frac{1}{11} \text{ of } 2\frac{1}{4}}{1\frac{7}{8} + \left(1\frac{1}{4} - \frac{1}{8}\right)}$$

$$= \frac{3\frac{10}{11} - 1\frac{1}{11} \text{ of } 2\frac{1}{4}}{1\frac{7}{8} + \left(1\frac{2-1}{8}\right)} \qquad \text{(work out brackets first)}$$

$$= \frac{3\frac{10}{11} - \left(\frac{\cancel{12}^{3}}{11} \times \frac{9}{\cancel{4}_{1}}\right)}{1\frac{7}{8} + 1\frac{1}{8}} \qquad \text{(work out 'of')}$$

$$= \frac{3\frac{10}{11} - 2\frac{5}{11}}{1\frac{7}{8} + 1\frac{1}{8}} \qquad \text{(subtract)}$$

$$= \frac{1\frac{10-5}{11}}{2\frac{7+1}{8}} \qquad \text{(add)}$$

$$= \frac{1\frac{5}{11}}{2\frac{8}{8}}$$

$$= 1\frac{5}{11} \div \frac{3}{1} \qquad \text{(divide)}$$

$$= \frac{16}{11} \times \frac{1}{3} = \frac{16}{33}$$

EXERCISE 15

1. $\dfrac{\left(2\frac{1}{2} + 1\frac{1}{4}\right) \times 3\frac{3}{8}}{1\frac{1}{2}}$

2. $\left(\frac{2}{8} - \frac{3}{24}\right) \div \left(\frac{5}{7} \text{ of } \frac{14}{20} + \frac{2}{8} \div \frac{2}{6}\right)$

3. $\dfrac{\frac{1}{3} \div \frac{3}{9} \text{ of } 2\frac{1}{4}}{\frac{3}{4} + \frac{7}{12}}$

Percentages

The words *per cent* mean per hundred. Hence, a century in cricket is 100 runs. The original century consisted of 100 men in the Roman Army, commanded by a *cent*urion. Each century in history is made up of 100 years. In America one *cent* is one hundredth part of a dollar. Getting more complicated, a *cent*al is a weight of 100 lbs used for corn, and a *cent*avo is one hundredth of a peso (South Amercian currency). A *cent*ennial celebrates someone or something that has lived or lasted 100 years or a hundredth anniversary. *Cent*igrade temperature is divided into 100 degrees from freezing point 0° to boiling point 100°. A *cent*ipede has (roughly!) 100 legs, and so on.

A percentage will *always* relate to 100. So, if we say 50% of the eggs are bad it means that out of every 100 eggs you will find 50 that are bad. With a percentage as simple as that we usually convert it to a fraction and say that half the eggs are bad. In fact, all percentages can be converted into fractions by simply dividing the percentage into 100. Thus 25% becomes $\frac{1}{4}$ (since $100 \div 25 = 4$), 10% would be $\frac{1}{10}$, and $12\frac{1}{2}\%$ would be $\frac{1}{8}$ (because $8 \times 12\frac{1}{2} = 100$).

Everyone in business uses percentages in some way or other, as do ordinary people in their daily life, so please do not be frightened by them! They are simplicity itself as you will find. Some of the uses for percentages are as follows.

Discount. This can be *trade* or *cash* and is used to indicate a reduction in price usually expressed as a percentage of the price, e.g. a new dress costs £25 less 5% discount for cash.

Commission. A payment made usually to a salesman calculated as a percentage of the value of the goods or services that have been sold, e.g. a waitress may earn an extra 5% on her earnings for all wine sales over a certain amount.

Interest. When money is lent to a borrower the amount of interest to be paid is calculated yearly as a percentage of the sum.

Depreciation. This is the reduction in the value of a possession or asset, and it is often expressed as a percentage of its original price, e.g. a new car depreciates by 10% the moment it is put on the road.

Examinations. Marks awarded are often given as a percentage of the total possible marks, e.g. a mark of 45 out of 60 gives a percentage mark of 75%. Similarly the number of candidates that pass may be given as a percentage of the total number of candidates.

Down Payments. When an article is bought on hire purchase or a house is bought, a deposit is asked for and this is usually given as a percentage of the full price, e.g. you would need £1750 as a down payment of 10% for a new house costing £17 500.

Increases in Salary, Wages, Cost of Living, etc. All of these are usually expressed as a percentage, e.g. the cost of living has increased by 10% since July.

Profit and Loss. When goods are sold the amount of profit or loss may be given as a percentage. This may be a percentage of the cost price or, as is more usual in business, it may be a percentage of SP (selling price).

VAT. This is a tax added to specified goods and services. At the time of writing it is 15% of cost price, e.g. a bill of £28.50 + VAT amounts to £32.78.

Dividends. When a company distributes its profits the shareholders are usually given a dividend which is expressed as a percentage of the capital, e.g. you may read, 'Metrotrust gave their shareholders a much higher dividend this year'. If you paid £2 a share and your dividend was 7p your percentage dividend or return would be $3\frac{1}{2}\% \left(\frac{7}{200} \times \frac{100}{1} \right)$. Note that this is called a dividend because it is the amount to be divided by the number of shares issued.

Working out percentages

Working out percentages can be done by two methods.

Method 1
Suppose we want to find a percentage of some other figure, for example 8% of £24.20.

In this case £24.20 is equivalent to 100%.

Therefore if 100% is equal to £24.20 then 1% must equal $\frac{£24.20}{100}$.

(N.B. Don't try to work this out yet.)

Now if $1\% = \frac{24.20}{100}$, then 8% must be 8 times as big or mathematically $\frac{24.20}{100} \times 8$ which equals $\frac{193.6}{100} = £1.936$.

Looking at all that, you can formulate a rule. If you want to know a percentage of another figure, then: *multiply by that percentage and divide by 100.*

EXERCISE 16

Work out the following percentages:

1. 14% of 67.78.
2. 32% of 43.70
3. 22% of 786.43
4. $16\frac{1}{2}$% of 44.66
5. 15% of £12.80
6. 60% of 30.60
7. 33% of £1765
8. 5% of £12.05

Method 2

The second method of working out percentages is when we wish to compare two figures. It is easier to understand the relationship of two figures if we represent this relationship as a percentage. Suppose we want to know what percentage 22.40 is of 86.40.

In this case we say that 86.40 is equal to 100%.

Therefore if 86.40 = 100% then 1 must equal $\frac{100}{86.40}$%.

(Once again don't try to work this out yet.)

Now if $1 = \frac{100}{86.40}$% then 22.40 must be 22.40 times as much, i.e.

$$\frac{100}{86.40} \times 22.40\%$$

$$= \frac{2240}{86.40}\%$$

$$= 25.93\%$$

From the above we can formulate the second rule:

$$\text{Percentage} = \frac{\text{Part}}{\text{Whole}} \times 100 \text{ or } \frac{\text{Smaller figure}}{\text{Larger figure}} \times 100.$$

EXERCISE 17

1. What percentage is 53.80 of 162.60?

2. What percentage is 23.42 of 88.78?

For the following you will need to look around and ask some questions:

3. What percentage of your group is female?

4. What percentage of your group come on the bus in the morning?

5. What percentage of your group want to end up working in hotels?

6. What percentage of your group work regularly at the weekend in catering?

25

7. What percentage of your college year is following a City and Guilds course?

8. What percentage of your group drink beer?

9. What percentage of your class went on to further study?

10. What percentage of your group has a motor cycle?

Quick revision for percentages

(i) Percentages are fractions with a denominator of 100.

(ii) To change a fraction to a percentage multiply by 100.

(iii) To change a percentage into a fraction divide it by 100.

(iv) To find the percentage of a quantity: (a) convert percentage to a fraction; (b) multiply the quantity by the fraction.

(v) Gross profit = turnover − cost price.

(vi) Net profit = gross profit − overheads.

(vii) Discount = selling price × $\dfrac{\text{percentage discount}}{100}$.

EXERCISE 18

1. If the weekly cost of living rises from £24.00 by 7%, what will the new weekly cost be?

2. If you dine out at a restaurant and the bill comes to £12.46, what will it be when a $12\frac{1}{2}$% service charge has been added?

3. If the price of a packet of cigarettes rises from 47 p to 52 p, what is the percentage increase?

4. If your hotel has 54 rooms and in one night lets 41, what is the percentage room occupancy?

5. If 236 students sit an examination and 194 pass, what is the percentage pass rate?

6. If 16.7% of a group of 24 students smoke, what is the actual number?

7. If you receive a 9% share of the pool of tips and in a week the pool was £87.95, what was your share?

8. If your weekly wage was £64, what would your take-home pay be if you remove 32% income tax?

9. A restaurant has 35 covers and in one night 42 people eat in the restaurant. What is the percentage occupancy?

10. If your annual salary is £1500 plus 5% commission on sales and the sales last year totalled £45470, what was your total income?

Converting decimals and fractions to percentages

A percentage is merely a fraction in which the quantity is given in hundreds, so to change a vulgar fraction or a decimal fraction to a percentage simply multiply by 100 and add the % sign.

Examples

(1) $\frac{1}{2} = \frac{1}{2} \times \frac{100}{1}\% = \frac{100}{2} = 50\%$

(2) $1\frac{3}{4} = \frac{7}{\cancel{4}_1} \times \frac{\cancel{100}^{25}}{1}\% = 175\%$

(3) $0.125 = 0.125 \times 100\% = 12.5\%$, i.e. move the point 2 places to the right.

(4) $3.875 = 3.875 \times 100\% = 387.5\%$, i.e. move the point 2 places to the right.

EXERCISE 19

Express the following as percentages. (Use fractions of percentages rather than decimals, i.e. write $6\frac{1}{2}\%$ rather than 6.5%.)

1. 0.010	2. 0.375	3. 2.75	4. $\frac{1}{8}$
5. $\frac{1}{20}$	6. $\frac{1}{3}$	7. $\frac{1}{6}$	8. $\frac{3}{8}$

Converting percentages to decimals and fractions

To change a percentage to a fraction or decimal fraction all that needs to be remembered is that percentages are hundredths.

Examples

(1) $75\% = \frac{\cancel{75}^3}{\cancel{100}_4} = \frac{3}{4}$

(2) $15\% = \frac{\cancel{15}^3}{\cancel{100}_{20}} = \frac{3}{20}$

(3) $8\% = \frac{\cancel{8}^2}{\cancel{100}_{25}} = \frac{2}{25}$

27

To change percentages to decimal form move point two places to left.

Examples

(1) $16\% = \dfrac{16}{100} = 0.16$

(2) $28.5\% = \dfrac{28.5}{100} = \dfrac{285}{1000} = 0.285$

EXERCISE 20

1. Express in fraction form:

   (a) 75%   (b) 18%   (c) 40%   (d) $6\frac{1}{4}\%$

   (e) 60%   (f) $6\frac{2}{3}\%$ (g) $12\frac{1}{2}\%$ (h) $17\frac{1}{2}\%$

2. Express in decimal form:

   (a) 60%   (b) 11%   (c) 80%   (d) 1%
   (e) 7%   (f) 30%   (g) 78%   (h) 50%
   (i) 10%   (j) 85%

3. Give the values for the blank spaces in this table:

Vulgar fraction	Decimal fraction	Percentage %
$\dfrac{2}{3}$	0.66	$66\frac{2}{3} = 66.67$
	0.43	
		60
$\dfrac{1}{20}$		
	0.75	
		$12\frac{1}{2} = 12.5$
	0.84	
$\dfrac{3}{8}$		

Some short cuts for special cases

If a required percentage is equivalent to a fraction with a numerator of one, then divide by the denominator.

Examples

(1) 50% $= \frac{50}{100} = \frac{1}{2}$, divide by 2

(2) 20% $= \frac{20}{100} = \frac{1}{5}$, divide by 5

(3) 10% $= \frac{10}{100} = \frac{1}{10}$, divide by 10

(4) 5% $= \frac{5}{100} = \frac{1}{20}$, divide by 20

(5) 1% $= \frac{1}{100}$, divide by 100

In the following exercise all the percentages are equivalent to simple fractions, and you can use these fractions to work out the answers.

EXERCISE 21

Find the following percentages, giving your results to the nearest penny:

1. 50% of £76.84
2. 25% of £108.20
3. 10% of £370
4. $33\frac{1}{3}$% of £51.75
5. 1% of £14632
6. $12\frac{1}{2}$% of £16.16

Other, more difficult, examples can also be worked out using fractions. Always try to work in powers of 10 to ease the calculation.

Examples

(1) Find $2\frac{1}{2}$% £146.65 $\left(2\frac{1}{2}\% = \frac{1}{40}, 40 = 4 \times 10\right)$.

        Step 1: Divide by 10 mentally = £14.665, move point 1 place to left

        Step 2: Divide by 4   = £3.666

                            = £3.67 to nearest penny.

(2) Find 5% of £78.83 $\left(5\% = \frac{1}{20}, 20 = 2 \times 10\right)$.

        Step 1: Divide by 10 mentally = £7.883, move point 1 place to left

        Step 2: Divide by 2   = £3.941

                            = £3.94 to nearest penny.

(3)   Find 6% of £478.75 $\left(6\% = \dfrac{6}{100},\text{ so divide by 100 and multiply by 6}\right)$.

Step 1: Divide by 100 mentally = £4.7875, move point 2 places to left

Step 2: Multiply by 6   = £28.7250

                        = £28.73 to nearest penny.

(4)   Find $\frac{1}{2}$% of £2345.50 $\left(\frac{1}{2}\% = 1\% \div 2,\text{ so divide by 100, then divide by 2}\right)$.

Step 1: Divide by 100 mentally = £23.4550, move point 2 places to left

Step 2: Divide by 2   = £11.7275

                        = £11.73 to nearest penny.

(5)   Find $7\frac{1}{2}$% of £127.35 $\left(7\frac{1}{2}\% = \dfrac{7}{100}\text{ and }\dfrac{\frac{1}{2}}{100},\text{ so divide by 100 (a), and}\right.$

divide by 2 to find $\frac{1}{2}$% (b), then multiply (a) by 7 and add to (b) .

Step 1: Divide by 100 mentally = £1.2735

Step 2: Divide by 2 mentally   = £0.63675

Step 3: Multiply answer to

       Step 1 by 7   = £8.9145

Step 4: Add Step 2 and Step 3 = £9.55125

                        = £9.55 to nearest penny.

EXERCISE 22

Find the following percentages, giving your results to the nearest penny:

1. $4\frac{1}{2}$% of £198

2. 3% of £234.50

3. 2% of £4321.50

4. 1% of £123.25

5. $\frac{1}{2}$% of £3368.06

6. $5\frac{1}{2}$% of £500.26

2
The Use of a Calculator

Introduction

The silicon chip is here to stay! No doubt, in the next ten years we will see considerable further development. As this book is being written, there is talk of the possibility of a calculator which will not only translate a foreign language but also show us how to pronounce it. Perhaps there will be a special calculator for caterers programmed to give the exact costings of dishes and budgeted gross profits. But this is in the future! How can we calculate our sums today?

Which calculator?

There are many different types of calculator on the market (some will also play music to you and wake you up in the morning) but accuracy and reliability must be of first importance. Accuracy on all calculators can be checked, before purchasing, quite easily. Simply feed the following calculation into the machine:

$123 \times 456 \div 789 =$

The answer should be: 71.087452 (or perhaps 71.087453).

If the calculator does not produce the above answer, look for another! If the calculator is mathematically correct, then look at the functions the machine is capable of doing. All calculators will cope with the four prime functions: *addition, subtraction, multiplication* and *division*; and, since these are the most used functions, check that they operate with algebraic logic. By that we mean that the machine will function in the same way you would either speak a problem or write a problem. In the first calculation given above, the numbers and key functions should be depressed in the order given — that is algebraic logic!

Now, whilst a calculator which copes only with the four prime functions does have considerable use, one which will cope with additional functions can be bought for very little extra outlay. We have already seen in Chapter 1 the importance of percentages, and a calculator which has a percentage key on it would certainly be an advantage. However, many machines have a percentage key which does not operate in the way the user would think it should. Look for a calculator which has a percentage key which also works with algebraic logic, and check it with the following calculation:

$$100 + 10\% = 110$$

Again, the keys should be depressed *exactly* as written above, some machines will give you an answer of: 10 and some will give a most peculiar answer. The best one to buy would be the one which gives 110 as the answer. If the machine being tested gives 110 then try the calculation in reverse and see if the logic works both ways. That is:

$$100 - 10\% = 90$$

If it does, then so far, so good! For most calculations the calculator is now acceptable.

Using the keys

A machine which will store information in the form of a memory will be more useful to the operator. The keys needed are: a *memory entry* or *memory store key* (**M**) a *memory recall key* (**MR**), a *memory cancel key* (**MC**) (sometimes the cancel function works on the basis of depressing the memory key twice), *a key to add to the memory* (**M +**), and *a key to subtract from the memory* (**M −**). Test the calculator with the following calculation:

$$10\ \textbf{M} + 15\ \textbf{M} + 20\ \textbf{M} - (\textbf{MR}) = 5.$$

Once again, the keys should be depressed in the order given above. If the answer held by the memory is not 5 then the machine will not be as much use to you.

When using a calculator the operator often finds that he has entered a figure incorrectly and would like to remove it without having to start the whole calculation from the beginning. The calculator should, therefore, have a key facility for doing this. Many of the cheaper calculators complete this function by instructing the operator to depress the **C** (clear key) *once* to remove an incorrect calculation and *twice* to clear the machine. The problem with this type of operation is that the operator runs the risk of removing the entire calculation if he forgets that he has depressed the **C** clear key once. It is much better to have a separate clear error key. If the machine being checked has this facility it will probably be marked **CE**. Check the machine with the following calculation:

$$15 + 25 + 50\ \textbf{CE} = 40$$

Once again, if the answer is not correct, test it again to make sure, and then, if it is still incorrect, do not buy!

Most of the more efficient calculators will have some form of a constant built into the machine. The constant works both within the function (addition, subtraction, division and multiplication) and within the number. Some machines have a specific constant key (usually marked **K**) and some are automatic.

The easiest type is the automatic. Check your machine to see if it has a built-in automatic constant by feeding it the following information:

$$10 \times 2 = 20$$

The machine should now have the (10 ×) as the constant; which means that if the operator depresses the key 5 and then = an answer of 50 should be display. If, after depressing the 5 key the answer on pressing the = is 10 then the machine does have a built in constant but it accepts the second function and number. The constant, once established, will operate for any of the prime or secondary functions. Try the following calculation:

$$100 \div 5 = 20$$
$$50 = 10$$
$$80 = 16$$

Remember to depress the keys in the order written above.

If the machine being tested has all the above functions, then it only remains to be seen whether it is reliable. By 'reliable' we mean the machine will not let us down. How is the machine powered? Some calculators work with normal calculator batteries, some with the tiny hearing-aid type of battery, and some from the mains supply through a transformer. The calculator which operates off normal small transistor batteries generally has an operating life of about 24 hours of constant use. This means that it will begin to lose power within about two to three weeks of normal use. This tends to be inconvenient, and it always seems to be at a time when the shops are closed that the batteries 'run out'!

The machine which runs off the mains supply, through a transformer, is only inconvenient in as much as the operator must carry the transformer about. This hardly makes the calculator a 'pocket' calculator.

Probably the best type of machine to purchase is the type which operates using the hearing-aid type of battery. These usually last for approximately one year and towards the end of their life most reliable machines will let the operator know that the batteries need changing by some form of display indication, such as a small (**b**) appearing on the display. The batteries can then be changed at the operator's convenience.

Having checked all the functions listed above, and so long as the operator is happy with the size of the machine (not too small — errors are more easily made; nor too large — difficulty to carry comfortably) and the type of display (easy and clear to read in all lights), then go ahead and purchase the calculator. In 1988, a machine which includes all the above functions and characteristics could be purchased for under £5.

There are many other varieties of calculator and the operator should purchase the one which will suit his needs best. If the operator is going to be involved in statistical work, then a machine can be purchased with square root keys, standard deviation keys, log keys, anti-log keys and so on.

Do not buy a machine just because it looks pretty or is going to impress somebody else.

Some simple rules

In describing, above, which calculator to buy, it has been explained how to use the calculator. However, in addition, there are one or two rules which the operator should abide by. These are:

(i)   Never rely completely on the answer the machine gives. Always work out a rough answer *before* the machine displays it.

(ii)   If the machine displays an answer you are not too sure about, start the entire calculation again and check it.

(iii) Do not let calculators make you lazy! They were not specifically designed as adding machines. In fact, most people can add up a column of figures faster that an operator can feed the same figures into a calculator.

(iv)   Do not use calculators for very simple calculations.

If you want to practise exercises on the calculator, try any of the exercises in this book. But remember – calculators can make you lazy and you may not always have one handy in the kitchen!

3
Systems of Measurement

Introduction

In many countries the units of weight, measures and currency have multiples, divisions and sub-divisions on a decimal basis. Some countries, e.g. France, use a complete metric system for currency, length, weight and temperature. Others only use part of the metric system. For example, the USA has a decimal coinage ($1 = 100 cents) but does not use metric weights. Since joining the EEC the UK is gradually moving to a full metric system. This means that we must know how to convert currency and other units both quickly and accurately. Certain units in hotel catering operations are used more often than others, and this chapter will concentrate only on these.

EXERCISE 23

Can you do the following quiz?

1. Which is the heavier:

   1 tonne   or   1 ton?

2. You need 2 litres of water. Would you fetch it in a:

   mug   or   milk bottle   or   pail?

3. If our temperature was taken and the thermometer reading was 37 °C, would you feel:

   normal   or   feverish   or   seriously ill?

4. If the recipe says 8 oz flour, which is the nearest weight in grams:

   175 g   or   200 g   or   225 g?

5. If the label suggests that the garment be washed in hand-hot water, what temperature would you use:

   35 °C   or   110 °C   or   212 °C?

6. Ladies, if your hip measurement was 102 cm and your bust 97 cm, what size dress would you wear:

   12   or   14   or   16?

7. For each curtain 6 ft of material is required. To allow for turnings you need to buy 13 ft. So you buy how many metres:

   3   or   4   or   5   or   6?

8. Which tin of paint will go the further:

   1 litre   or   1 quart?

9. The instructions say 'allow 12 cm'. If you did not have a metric measure, how much would you allow in inches:

   $3\frac{1}{2}$ or $4\frac{3}{4}$ or $5\frac{1}{4}$?

10. The basic height for kitchen worktops is 900 mm. (Builders and furniture-makers work in millimetres and metres.) What is this on the metric scale:

    9 cm   or   9 m   or   90 cm?

    What is it on the imperial scale:

    $3\frac{1}{2}$ inches   or   27 ft   or   3 ft?

11. A signpost on a footpath indicates 16 km to the village. How far will you have to walk:

    6 miles   or   8 miles   or   10 miles?

12. You are allowed 35 kilograms as free baggage on your holiday flight. If your case weighs 5 stones on your bathroom scales, will you have to pay excess baggage:

    Yes   or   No?

13. If a block of butter weighs 454 grams, would you be buying:

    1 lb   or $\frac{1}{2}$ lb   or $\frac{1}{4}$ lb?

14. The medicine bottle label says take 2 teaspoons every four hours. Does the standard medicine spoon hold:

    5 ml   or   10 ml   or   25 ml?

15. If you needed 10 gallons of petrol in France, how many litres would you ask for:

    10   or   20   or   45   or   50?

16. When shopping you see two special offers for biscuits:

    175 grams for 23 p   or   250 grams for 39 p

    Which is the better buy?

17. Two tubes of toothpaste contain:

    45 cc   and   25 ml

    Which is the larger?

18. If you were ordering new table napkins for the restaurant, would you order:

    45 cm squares   or   60 cm squares   or   90 cm squares?

19. Does an ordinary bottle of wine contain:

    70 cl   or   75 cc   or   75 ml?

20. If the recipe said use 20 fluid ounces, how may millilitres would you use:

    1000   or   500   or   200?

When you have read this chapter, try again and you should get them all correct!

Metric weight

Most of the commodities purchased in the UK are now sold in metric quantities. Some exceptions are fresh meat and vegetables. The main units used in catering are the kilogram (abbreviated kg) and the gram (abbreviated g officially, but look out for gm and gms!).

Thus

$$1000 \text{ grams} = 1 \text{ kilogram}$$

$$500 \text{ grams} = \frac{1}{2} \text{ kilogram} = 0.500 \text{ kilogram}$$

$$250 \text{ grams} = \frac{1}{4} \text{ kilogram} = 0.250 \text{ kilogram}$$

$$100 \text{ grams} = \frac{1}{10} \text{ kilogram} = 0.100 \text{ kilogram}$$

A decimal point is used to separate the grams from the kilogram, e.g.

$$3.200 \text{ kg} = 3200 \text{ g} = 3 \text{ kg} + 200 \text{ g} = 3.2 \text{ kg}$$

When working in metric weights in the kitchen it is usual to leave the third zero after the point on the end. This means that when you see 3.200 kg you immediately recognise that there are 3 kilograms and 200 grams in the weight.

Conversion from imperial weights to metric weights

When changing imperial measure to metric it is necessary to have a *conversion factor*. Unfortunately nobody will agree the best equivalent to use. Some organisations use 25 grams equal to 1 ounce; others use 30 grams equal to 1 ounce.

The difficulty arises because 1 ounce actually equals 28.35 g. When you are converting a recipe it does not really matter *which* conversion factor you use so long as you are *consistent*! The authors both prefer using 25 grams to the ounce because this is much easier and more convenient. For example, for many foods one portion is 4 ounces and this works out as 100 g, which is *very* useful when you are working out an order and when you want to work out nutritional content for which the tables use portion sizes of 100 g! (Note that extra care must be taken when converting a recipe containing both liquid and solid ingredients. This problem will be dealt with later in this chapter.)

Examples

(1) Crumble Ingredients for Apple Crumble:

Ingredient	Quantity	Conversion factor	Metric quantity
Flour	4 oz	25 g = 1 oz (25 × 4)	100 g
Margarine	2 oz	25 g = 1 oz (25 × 2)	50 g
Granulated sugar	2 oz	25 g = 1 oz (25 × 2)	50 g

(2) Convert the following recipe for Almond Curl to metric quantities:

$2\frac{1}{2}$ oz margarine

$2\frac{1}{2}$ oz caster sugar

$1\frac{1}{2}$ oz plain flour

2 oz flaked almonds

You will notice that $\frac{1}{2}$ oz is repeatedly used here. This gives a $12\frac{1}{2}$ g equivalent. Usually you would round this up to the nearest 5 g.

Ingredient	Quantity	Conversion factor	Metric quantity
Margarine	$2\frac{1}{2}$ oz	25 g = 1 oz	65 g
Caster sugar	$2\frac{1}{2}$ oz	$2\frac{1}{2} \times 25 = 62\frac{1}{2}$ g	65 g
Plain flour	$1\frac{1}{2}$ oz	$1\frac{1}{2} \times 25 = 37\frac{1}{2}$ g	40 g
Flaked almonds	2 oz	$2 \times 25 = 50$ g	50 g

The use of columns may appear very basic, but it does mean that the quantities are easily checked and mistakes spotted.

Metric capacity

Because a large number of the measures found in kitchens are scaled both in imperial measure (pints) and metric scales, the majority of people still tend to think of liquid in pints and fractions of pints.

The general conversion factors of capacity are even more debatable than weight varying between 1 litre $= 1\frac{3}{4}$ pints (pt), or more usually 1 litre $= 2$ pints, 1 fluid ounce (fl oz) $= 25$ millilitres (ml). This means that if the lower figure of 25 g $= 1$ oz is used, too much liquid can be added to the mixture, thus altering the consistency. So if you are using a recipe that has been converted from imperial to metric, always add the liquid sparingly and a little at a time. It is always possible to add extra liquid and correct the consistency but *very* difficult to remove it. The measurement is not so critical for most sauces and soups. However, it does give more substance to the idea of thinking entirely in metric and *never* using metric weight and imperial liquid measurement in the same recipe unless the exact quantity is worked out, e.g.

$$586 \text{ ml} = 1 \text{ pt} = 20 \text{ fl oz}$$
$$146.5 \text{ ml} = \frac{1}{4} \text{ pt} = 5 \text{ fl oz}$$

This last figure will explain why some recipes use 150 ml $= \frac{1}{4}$ pt, and this is the amount recommended if 30 g $= 1$ oz is used for the conversion of dry ingredients.

$$1000 \text{ ml} = 1 \text{ litre} = 1 \text{ kg} = 1000 \text{ g}$$

Fortunately for the purposes of calculating metric recipe conversions the quantity is not so critical except in the pastry section, as long as the method of finding the quantity is known and can be worked out, and the right conversion factors used.

Examples

(1) Find the metric equivalents for Watercress Soup, using 25 g $= 1$ oz and 25 ml $= 1$ fl oz.

      2 bunches water cress

      1 oz margarine or butter

      2 oz onions

      3 oz potato

      $\frac{1}{2}$ pt milk

      $\frac{1}{2}$ pt chicken stock

      $\frac{1}{8}$ pt cream

Ingredient	Imperial quantity	Conversion	Metric quantity
Watercress	2 bunches	Same	2 bunches
Margarine	1 oz	1×25	25 g
Potato	3 oz	3×25	75 g
Onion	2 oz	2×25	50 g
Milk	$\frac{1}{2}$ pt	10×25	250 ml
Chicken stock	$\frac{1}{2}$ pt	10×25	250 ml
Cream	$\frac{1}{8}$ pt	$2\frac{1}{2} \times 25$	$62\frac{1}{2}$ ml

(2)   Using same recipe but use conversion factor 30 g = 1 oz and $\frac{1}{4}$ pt = 150 ml. (Note the abbreviations.)

Ingredient	Imperial quantity	Conversion	Metric quantity
Watercress	2 bunches	Same	2 bunches
Margarine	1 oz	1×30	30 g
Potato	3 oz	3×30	90 g
Onion	2 oz	2×30	60 g
Milk	$\frac{1}{2}$ pt	150×2	300 ml
Chicken stock	$\frac{1}{2}$ pt	150×2	300 ml
Cream	$\frac{1}{8}$ pt	$150 \div 2$	75 ml

In some metric recipes and also in imperial recipes, smaller measures are given in various sized spoons. The British Standards Institute have a standard for these based on 15 ml = 1 tablespoon (or tbs) and 5 ml = 1 teaspoon. It would be sensible in practice to use these spoons remembering that they are always taken as *level* measure and the special spoons are to be recommended. If, when converting and 'bulking up' recipes for large scale use, the millilitre quantity is remembered for liquid, it is quicker to measure a liquid quantity than to measure out 20 tablespoons of a commodity.

Example
Convert to metric quantities this recipes for Custard Sauce:

$1\frac{1}{2}$ tablespoons custard powder

2 tablespoons sugar

$\frac{1}{2}$ pt milk

Ingredient	Quantity	Conversion	Metric quantity
Custard powder	$1\frac{1}{2}$ tbs	$1\frac{1}{2} \times 15$ ml	2×10 ml spoons
Sugar	2 tbs	2×15 ml	2×15 ml spoons
Milk	$\frac{1}{2}$ pt	$\frac{1}{2} \times 20 \times 25$ ml	250 ml

EXERCISE 24

1. Find some recipes using imperial measure and convert them to metric measure. State the conversion factors you used and explain why you used them.

2. Find some recipes in metric measure and see if you can guess what conversion factors have been used.

Wine and carafe

The Sale of Wine Order (1976) has now stated that wine by the carafe must be sold in Government stamped carafes of 25 cl or multiples of half a litre, or else a measuring device, Government-stamped, must be used at the time of the purchase. The wine poured into the measure and then transferred to a carafe in front of the customer. The Order also states that a carafe should be capable of being completely emptied at an angle of 120°. The only design so far produced to do this looks like a hospital bottle, and when filled with white wine its presence on the table is far from aesthetic! Although there is now an Order which protects the customer against racketeers serving wine in a carafe, the sale of wine by the glass is now wide open to abuse, as previously the amount of the wine in the glass and its price had to be stated. Now one is able to advertise a glass of wine at a stated price but the glass size or capacity need not be revealed to the customer.

Metric length

Metric linear measurements are based on the metre, which is equivalent to 39.37 inches, and the kilometre which is 1000 metres and equal to 0.621 miles or very nearly $\frac{5}{8}$ mile. Metric lengths are used in many different areas of relevance to the: caterer:

(i) In the building trade, i.e. for kitchen fittings and bedroom conversions etc., the units used are the metre and the millimetre (one-thousandth of a metre), but the centimetre (one-hundredth of a metre) is not commonly used.

(ii) Sizes of bain-marie trays for use in ovens, refrigerators and bain-maries are given in the 'Gastronorm' tin sizes. There are $\frac{1}{1}, \frac{1}{2}, \frac{1}{4}, \frac{1}{6}, \frac{1}{8}, \frac{1}{3}$. These are not to be read as fractions, but $\frac{1}{1}$ is the largest tray, and the bottom number indicates how many containers can be fitted into a space equal to the largest tray.

(iii) The standard height for equipment is 900 mm, the depth is 300 mm and the lengths of the units are multiples of 300, 500, 700 and 900 mm, so that straight runs can be made. These units are known as *modules*.

(iv) For beds and bed linen, a straight conversion is used. A single bed is 90 cm wide and a double bed of 4 foot 6 inches is 135 cm wide, the length being 190 cm. However, the bed linen is marked in cm (e.g. 180 cm × 260 cm) and then labelled 'suitable for a 3 foot bed'. Table linen has now gone almost completely metric, the old 36 inch square cloth becoming one metre square, though some manufacturers are still using the old looms and giving approximations. It is sensible to check current practice before ordering. When buying fabric and carpeting you will find both units are available and the price should be checked per unit purchased. The supplier will cut to the nearest 10 cm if metric units are used, $\frac{1}{4}$ yard if he is still using imperial measure.

(v) Distances between towns are increasingly in kilometres and speed is being measured in kilometres per hour. As we have already noted, 1 km is approximately $\frac{5}{8}$ mile, or 5 miles represents approximately 8 kilometres, so 30 miles per hour in the metric system is approximately 50 kilometres per hour (please inform your French chef is he is a reckless driver!).

The Centigrade scale of temperature

The temperatures on the majority of electric ovens, central heating boilers etc. are now measured in degrees Celsius, which means they are measured on the Centigrade scale. Weather reports also use this scale nowadays as do clinical thermometers. Again it is advisable to try and think metric all the time; some people simply won't understand if you tell them that the temperature of the sea water is 25 °C — it doesn't mean anything to them and they need a quick guide to relate it to something they know.

Converting Fahrenheit to Centigrade and Centigrade to Fahrenheit

The table below shows how you can convert from one scale to another. The quick methods are useful in emergencies or when you do not need a very accurate answer but if you want to convert temperatures to the nearest degree, use the accurate method.

	Converting °F → °C	Converting °C → °F
Very quick method for oven temperatures	(1) Halve	(2) Double
Quick method for lower temperatures	(3) Subtract 30, then halve	(4) Double, then add 30
Accurate method for all temperatures	(5) Subtract 32 then multiply by $\frac{5}{9}$	(6) Multiply by $\frac{9}{5}$, then add 32

Here are some examples of how to use these methods.

Examples

(1)   Mrs Beeton's recipe book recommends 400°F. My oven is in °C and there's panic in the kitchen. What temperature shall I use?

Answer: $\frac{400\,°F}{2} = 200°C$

(2)   The *Modern Cook Book* says 'roast at 220°C'. Gran's cooker is in °F. What shall I do?

Answer: roast at 220 × 2 = 440°F — which probably means 450°F on Gran's cooker.

43

COSTING AND CALCULATIONS FOR CATERING

(3)   It must be about 80 °F in the shade. What's that roughly in °C?

Answer: 80 − 30 = 50. $\frac{50}{2}$ = 25. So it's about 25 °C.

(4)   "The 'met' man says it's going to be 22 °C tomorrow. I can't understand these new temperatures, son. What is that – about 60 in the old scale?" (Son thinks: 22 × 2 = 44. 44 + 30 = 74.)

Answer: "No, it's going to be hot, Dad. About 74°F!"

(5)   The normal blood temperature is 98.4 °F. What is that in °C?

Answer: 98.4 − 32 = 66.4

$$66.4 \times \frac{5}{9} = 36.9 °C$$

(6)   The temperature in this room is 14 °C. What is that in °F to the nearest degree?

Answer: $14 \times \frac{9}{5} = 25.2$

25.2 + 32 = 57.2

= 57 °F   (to the nearest degree)

Now try the following exercise.

EXERCISE 25

1.   Convert each of the following oven temperatures very roughly to the other scale:
    (a) 450 °F   (b) 200 °C   (c) 350 °F   (d) 150 °C

2.   Convert each of the following temperatures to the other scale, using (i) the 'quick method' and (ii) the 'accurate method':
    (a) 30 °C   (b) 106 °F   (c) 100 °C   (d) 32 °F
    (e) 56 °C   (f) 450 °F   (g) − 40 °C   (h) − 2 °F

Foreign currency

When people travel from one country to another they must change their money into foreign currency. The relationship between one country's currency and another is measured by the *rate of exchange*. The current rates of exchange can always be found in the better daily newspapers or from the bank.

Example
Change £40 into Swiss francs when the rate of exchange is 3.46 Swiss francs to £1.

Answer = 40 × 3.46
= 138.4 Swiss francs

EXERCISE 26

1. Using the current rates of exchange, convert the following sterling amounts:
   - (a) £106 to Danish kroner
   - (b) £5.50 to Italian lire
   - (c) £38.90 to yen
   - (d) £1796 to riyals
   - (e) £196.25 to US dollars
   - (f) £212.50 to guilders
   - (g) £525 to Deutsche marks
   - (h) £59.20 to French francs

2. Now use current rates of exchange to prepare the following table to help you know the currency equivalents so that you can organise your Grand Tour of Europe

Country	Money unit	£1	50 p	10 p	5 p	1 p
				Exchange rate		
France	Franc					
Spain	Peseta					
Italy	Lira					
Portugal	Escudo					
W Germany	Deutsche mark					
Switzerland	Swiss franc					
Holland	Guilder					

To convert foreign currency to sterling *divide* by the rate of exchange.

Example
Change 1580 francs to sterling.

Answer: $\frac{1580}{8.80}$

= £179.55

EXERCISE 27

Using the current rates of exchange, change the following into sterling:

1. 2400 riyals
2. 8000 Danish kroner
3. 4380 roubles
4. 1750 yen

5. 5720 escudos **6.** 10 000 US dollars

7. 250 HK dollars **8.** 825 lire

It is sometimes useful to know the sterling equivalent of a currency unit. This is done by dividing the pound by the rate of exchange.

Examples

(1) 1 French franc $= \dfrac{100\ p}{8.8} = 11\dfrac{1}{2}$

(2) Swiss franc $= \dfrac{100\ p}{3.46} = 28.90\ p$

$= 29\ p$ to nearest penny

If the divisor is a large number as is the case with lire, divide it down.

Example

1750 lire	=	100 p
875 lire	=	50 p
87.5 lire	=	5 p
17.5 lire	=	1 p

EXERCISE 28

Find the sterling equivalent of the unit of currency in each of the following:

1. French franc **2.** yen **3.** riyal **4.** guilder

5. HK dollar **6.** escudo **7.** kroner **8.** peseta

Calculation of commodities bought by a price per kilogram

With the use of metric weights and capacity, invoices are calculated by the cost of a kilogram and when costing individual dishes you have to work out fractions of a kilogram. This operation can be carried out by 2 methods:

Method 1

By using a figure of $\dfrac{1}{100}$ of the kilogram price for 100 grams and $\dfrac{1}{100}$ of the kilogram price for 10 grams. In other words just move the point one or two places to the left, but remember always to work in pence not pounds.

Example

How much would it cost to buy 400 grams of fillet beef at £4.90 per kilogram?

Call the cost per kilogram	490 p
Then 100 grams cost 490 ÷ 10	49 p
So 400 grams costs 49 × 4	196 p
Total	£1.96 p

Method 2

If the quantities required are simple fractions, e.g. $500 \text{ g} = \frac{1}{2}$ kilogram and $250 \text{ g} = \frac{1}{4}$ kilogram, the above method need not be used as the cost per kilogram can be divided by the denominator of the fraction.

Example

How much would it cost to buy 500 grams of butter at £1.50 per kilogram?

1 kilogram costs £1.50

$\frac{1}{2}$ kilogram costs $\dfrac{£1.50}{2} = 75 \text{ p}$

To make the concept simpler follow the next section through and decide for yourself which method works best for you.

In the following exercise work the easier fractions of a kilogram using the fractional method and the quantities not easily made into fractions using the method based on tenths. The exercise has been worded using the many ways that goods are itemised on invoices. Therefore care must be taken in their interpretation, also whether the cost is per kilogram or half kilogram. Note must also be taken that when an item is written:

150 × 100 g pork chops at £2.60 per kilo

It means that 150 pork chops at 100 grams have been requested. To make the calculation, first find the total weight then multiply this by the cost.

Example

Weight of pork ordered is: $\dfrac{150 \times 100}{1000} \text{kg} = 15 \text{ kg}$

Cost of pork will be: $15 \times £2.60 = £39$

or

Cost of pork: $\dfrac{\overset{3}{\cancel{150}} \times \cancel{100}}{\cancel{1000}} \times \dfrac{\overset{13}{\cancel{260}}}{\underset{2}{\cancel{100}}} = £39$

47

EXERCISE 29

1. Calculate the following using simple fractions of a kilogram:

    (a)   5.250 kg at £1.80 per $\frac{1}{2}$ kg   (b)   0.050 kg at £5 per kilo

    (c) $1\frac{3}{4}$ kg at £3.75 per kilo   (d)   10.125 kg at 75 p per kilo.

2. Calculate the following using tenths and hundredths of a kilogram:

    (a)   1.375 kg at 62 p per kilo   (b)   2.340 kg at 10 p per $\frac{1}{2}$ kilo

    (c)   1.115 kg at £1.15 per $\frac{1}{2}$ kg   (d)   21 × 55 g at £1.80 per kilo.

3. Calculate the following, deciding for yourself which method to use:

    (a)   6.500 kg at 99 p per kg   (b)   3.150 kg at £187 per kilo

    (c)   30 × 75 g at £3.20 per kg   (d)   1.075 kg at 78 p per kilo.

The 24-hour clock

British Rail, the coach operators and all airlines use the 24-hour clock. This means that there is no need to distinguish between morning and afternoon by using the abbreviations a.m. and p.m. A minute after midnight is written as 00.01 or 00.01 hours and a minute after midday is written as 12.01 or 12.01 hours. The point in this figure does not mean one-tenth of an hour, but is used to denote the number of minutes past the hour.

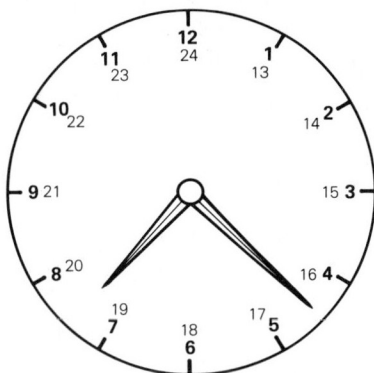

Alternatively 13.00–2400 hours may be shown in a different colour

The following examples show how to convert from one system to the other.

Examples

(1)   What is 8.30 a.m. on the 24-hour clock?

Put a zero before the 8 and remove the a.m.

Answer: 08.30 (hours)

(2)   What is 8.30 p.m. on the 24-hour clock?

Add 12 to the 8 and remove the a.m.
Answer: 20.30 (hours)

(3)   What is 12.20 a.m. on the 24-hour clock?

This is just after *midnight.*
Answer: 00.20 (hours)

(4)   What is 12.20 p.m. on the 24-hour clock?

This is just after *midday.*
Answer: 12.20 (hours)

(5)   What is 10.30 hours in a.m. or p.m.?

This is less than 12, so it is before midday (a.m.)
Answer: 10.30 a.m.

(6)   What is 19.30 hours in a.m. or p.m.?

This is more than 12, so it is after midday.
Subtract 12 and put p.m.
Answer: 7.30 p.m.

(7)   What is 00.45 hours in a.m. or p.m.?

This is just after *midnight.*
Answer: 12.45 a.m.

(8)   What is 12.45 hours in a.m. or p.m.?

This is just after *midday.*
Answer: 12.45 p.m.

EXERCISE 30

1.   Give the following times on the 24-hour clock:
   (a)   12.10 p.m.   (b)   6.35 a.m.   (c)   7.11 p.m.   (d)   9.27 a.m.
   (e)   10.30 p.m.   (f)   9.30 p.m.   (g)   2.16 a.m.   (h)   12.10 a.m.

2.   Give the following times in a.m. or p.m.:
   (a)   19.09 hours   (b)   12.55 hours   (c)   20.30 hours   (d)   22.12 hours
   (e)   20.05 hours   (f)   06.00 hours   (g)   17.05 hours   (h)   00.15 hours

4
Food Costing

Introduction

While the control of all aspects of commodities, equipment and liquor is critical for a successful catering operation, it is absolutely vital that the costing of a dish and its selling price, with relation to its production price, is accurately arrived at. However, it is the clever caterer who is prepared to gain his profits on the 'swings and roundabouts' give a customer value for money, and provide food that the customer wants at a price he is prepared to pay, who will be laughing all the way to the bank. This skill is something that cannot be taught but is acquired with experience. This experience could be painful and financially disastrous, so some guidelines are needed to prevent an increase in the number of bankruptcies in the catering trade and to replace this with a restaurant full of satisfied, well-fed, customers — and a millionaire owner!

The crux of this situation is threefold:

(i)   Good menu planning, making use of good buys, seasonal foods, attractive range of dishes that the customer wants.

(ii) Accurate sales forecasting linked with clever use of unused food.

(iii) The use of well-tried recipes that give a known yield which is understood by both kitchen and restaurant staff who have been trained in portion control.

Recipes are often guarded with great professional jealousy and handed down or not as the case may be. Dishes are given classical names and bear no resemblance to the original creation, in spite of the Trade Descriptions Act. Be this as it may, the importance of the recipe as far as food costing is concerned is that you should include all the ingredients used in the dish and cost and total them before deciding on the selling price. This is considerably aided by having a well planned costing sheet for each dish which is up-dated regularly. To help menu planning they could be colour-coded both for Dinner, Luncheon or Banqueting purposes, and also for price range.

For example, a Table d'hôte menu there could be a pink sheet for low-cost dishes, a blue sheet for medium-cost dishes and a green sheet for the most expensive dishes. It is useful to record on these sheets the skill required in preparation and the time required to make them. If the dish contains commodities liable to seasonal price fluctuations, you should either cost the dish for the commodity's high and low price or use an average price, but this would not be so satisfactory.

(Because of inflation the cost of food, in worked examples cannot be kept accurate. To obtain realistic costs, you should check commodity prices. It is a useful exercise to work out a costing sheet each month and see how price changes affect the selling price of a dish and the profit.)

Kitchen percentage

What kitchen percentage means

This percentage is also sometimes called the *food cost percentage*. This means that it is the cost of the food expressed as a percentage of the selling price (which we think of as representing 100%). We can write this definition in a formula:

$$\text{Food cost percentage or Kitchen percentage} = \frac{\text{Food cost}}{\text{Selling price}} \times 100$$

If you learn the formula, you will find it very easy to use.

Example

Coq au vin sells for £5. The food costs £2. What is the kitchen percentage?

Use the formula:

$$\text{Kitchen percentage} = \frac{\text{Food cost}}{\text{Selling price}} \times 100$$

$$= \frac{£2}{5} \times 100$$

$$= 40\%$$

EXERCISE 31

Find the kitchen percentage when a dish sells at:

1. £9.00 and costs £3.00   2. 75 p and costs 37 ½ p

3. 30 p and costs 12 p

Working out a selling price from kitchen percentage

Suppose you know the food cost and the kitchen percentage and want to find out the selling price. You can then use the formula:

$$\text{Selling price} = \frac{\text{Food cost}}{\text{Kitchen percentage}} \times 100$$

This is really the same formula as the one on page 51, but it has been written in a different way. It is worth learning because if you know both these formulae you can solve *all* your food costing-calculation problems!

Example

Steak and Kidney Pie costs 30 p to produce. If the food cost percentage is 30%, what is the selling price?

Use the formula:

$$\text{Selling price} = \frac{\text{Food cost}}{\text{Kitchen percentage}} \times 100$$

$$= \frac{30 \text{ p}}{30} \times 100$$

$$= 100 \text{ p} = £1$$

Sometimes you can use a short cut to find out the selling price. If there is a 50% kitchen percentage for example and you divide by 50%, this means you are dividing by $\frac{1}{2}$ or multiplying by 2.

Example

The food cost of ice-cream is 20 p with a 50% kitchen percentage. What is the selling price?

Selling price = 2 × 20 p = 40 p

Similarly with a 40% kitchen percentage you multiply the food cost by $2\frac{1}{2}$ to get the selling cost.

Example

Watercress Soup costs 20 p with a kitchen percentage of 40%. What is the selling price?

Selling price = $2\frac{1}{2}$ × 20 p = 50 p

EXERCISE 32

Find the selling prices (to the nearest penny) of the following dishes to show kitchen percentages of (a) 40%, (b) 45%, (c) 30%, (d) 50%.

1. Canard à l'orange, food cost £2.75.

2. Crème caramel, food cost 15 p.

3. Bread and Butter Pudding, food cost 22 p.

4. Navarin of Lamb, food cost 24 p.

What would you multiply the food cost by to get the selling price if the kitchen percentage was:

5. 25%   6. $33\frac{1}{3}$%?

The relationship between kitchen percentage, gross profit percentage and selling price

If it costs £2 to produce a dish and we wish to make £3 gross profit, the selling price is obviously £2 + £3 = £5. This means that we can always write a simple formula:

Selling price = Food cost + Gross profit

We always think of the selling price as 100%, so

100% = Food cost percentage + Gross profit percentage

or

100% = Kitchen percentage + Gross profit percentage

This means that if you are given kitchen percentage or the gross profit percentage, the other can be found by subtracting it from 100%.

53

Examples

(1)   Find the kitchen percentage if a gross profit percentage of 60% is required:

Kitchen percentage = 100% − 60% = 40%

(2)   Find the gross profit percentage if the kitchen percentage is 35%:

Gross profit percentage = 100% − 35% = 65%

EXERCISE 33

1. Find the gross profit percentage if the following kitchen percentages are achieved:

(a)   65%   (b)   30%   (c)   28%   (d)   38%   (e)   40%

2. Now find the kitchen percentage if the following gross profit percentages are required:

(a)   68%   (b)   70%   (c)   58%   (d)   45%   (e) $66\frac{2}{3}$%

Working out the gross profit percentage from the costs

There are two ways of doing this: either (Method 1) by working out the kitchen percentage and subtract from 100 or (Method 2) working out the gross profit and then expressing this as a percentage of the selling price. Studying the following examples should show you how both methods work out.

Example
A dish costs 16p and sells for 40p. What is the gross profit percentage?

Method 1

$$\text{Kitchen percentage} = \frac{\text{Food cost}}{\text{Selling price}} \times 100$$

$$= \frac{16}{40} \times 100$$

$$= 40\%$$

Gross profit percentage = 100% − 40%
= 60%

Method 2
You work out the profit first:

Profit = 40p − 16p = 24p

Now use the formula similar to the one for kitchen percentage

$$\text{Gross profit percentage} = \frac{\text{Gross profit}}{\text{Selling price}} \times 100$$

$$= \frac{24}{40} \times 100$$

$$= \frac{2400}{40}$$

$$= 60\%$$

Now try the following exercise using both methods.

EXERCISE 34

Find the gross profit percentage when a dish sells for:

1. 50 p and costs 10 p
2. 75 p and costs 25 p

3. £1.80 and costs £1.00

(Did you find one method easier than the other?)

Setting a target for kitchen percentage

In business we learn from experience what proportion of our total sales the profit needs to be in order to pay the expenses of the business and to leave enough over (surplus or net profit) to make the job worthwhile.

It is, therefore, essential that a target is set and actual results are compared with the target to determine the efficiency both in the kitchen and restaurant. One of these targets is the kitchen (or food cost) percentage.

On some occasions the target kitchen percentage will not be met: it could be more or it could be less. These fluctuations should be investigated as too high a gross profit percentage could be as problematical as too low a one. These fluctuations could be due to one or more of the following reasons:

(i)   Inefficiency in any area including book-keeping.

(ii)   Food prices rising and falling and costing sheets not adjusted.

(iii) Incorrect portion control.

(iv)   Theft.

(v)   Variations in customer demand.

It is very important that costs should be recorded accurately if kitchen percentages are to be met. To do this we need a costing sheet, and the details of this are given in the next section.

The costing sheet

A costing sheet could take the format shown in Figs. 1 and 2, though each establishment usually designs its own. The important point is that a costing sheet should be produced and used. The cost per portion is found by dividing the total cost by the number of portions the recipe is meant to yield. In the example shown in Fig. 2, if 100 portions are obtained then the food cost per portion will be 22.54 p, giving a selling price of 64 p based on a kitchen percentage of 35% (can you work this out?). If, however, because of:

(i)   bad portion control at the time of service,

(ii)   wasteful preparation of ingredients,

(iii)   poor quality of meat purchased,

(iv)   overcooking,

only 90 portions are obtained, then the portion cost would be

$$£\frac{22.54}{90} = 25 \tfrac{1}{2} \text{ p}$$

and the selling price should be, with 35% kitchen percentage, 71 p (without VAT). This could cause a loss of 7 p per portion and could mean a shortage of cash to pay the wages and other overheads.

It is important to note that if your kitchen is well organised, use can be made of kitchen 'left-overs'. For example, the dripping used is obtained as a result of rendering down meat fat, and the garnish can be made up of previously blanched vegetables from another meal, which may have been costed into another dish. This, of course, is sensible kitchen practice if the rules of hygiene and réchauffé are observed.

COSTING SHEET			
RECIPE			
Ingredient	*Quantity*	*Unit cost*	*Ingredient cost*
TOTAL			

Yield:
Wastage:
Cost per portion:
Seasonal variation cost — High:
                           Low:

Selling price for kitchen percentage
of 35%
    40%
    50%
    60%

Fig. 1. A costing sheet. If the sheet is to be used as a kitchen aid as well, the reverse side should contain the following information.

METHOD:

Size of baking tin:
No. of portions per container:
Portion size or equipment:

BAKING TEMPERATURE:

BAKING/COOKING TIME:

Usual production run:

COSTING SHEET			
RECIPE Navarin of Lamb			
Ingredient	*Quantity*	*Unit cost*	*Ingredient cost*
Neck of lamb	16¼ kg	1.12 kg	18.20
Carrot	3 kg	20 p kg	0.60
Onion	2¾ kg	20 p kg	0.55
Tomato puree	½ kg	50 p kg	0.25
Beans, French	2 kg	55 p kg	1.10
Peas, frozen	2 kg	55 p kg	1.10
Turnip	2 kg	20 p kg	0.40
Fat (dripping)	½ kg	16 p kg	0.08
Flour	¾ kg	12 p kg	0.09
Salt	50 g	20 p kg	0.01
Pepper	25 g	16 p/25 g	0.16
		TOTAL	£22.54

Yield: 100 portions	SELLING PRICE FOR kitchen percentage		
Wastage:	of	35%	64 p
Cost per portion: 22.54 p		40%	56 p
Seasonal variation cost — High: + 1.4 p per portion		50%	45 p
Low: − 0.50 p per portion		60%	38 p

Fig. 2. Example of a costing sheet filled in. Remember that the selling price for the kitchen percentage does not include VAT.

EXERCISE 35

1. Complete the costing sheet in Fig. 3 for Apple Flan (Flan aux pommes). Then:
    (a) Find the cost of ingredients for 1 Flan, to the nearest penny.
    (b) Calculate the average cost per portion.
2. Complete the costing sheet in Fig. 4 for Caramel Custard (Crème caramel).
    (a) Find the cost of ingredients for 40 portions.
    (b) Calculate the average cost per portion, to the nearest penny.
    (c) Show the average cost per portion when the price of large eggs is:
    (i) 5 ½ p   (ii) 5 p each   (iii) 6 ½ p each
3. Using your own recipes make costing sheets for and find cost per portion for 100 portions of:
    (a) Mushroom Soup   (b) Mixed Grill   (c) Apple Flan
4. Repeat Exercise 3 for 25 portions of:
    (a) Lemon Soufflé   (b) Roast Beef and Yorkshire Pudding
    (c) Fresh Fruit Salad.

COSTING SHEET

RECIPE   Flan aux pommes

Ingredient	Quantity	Unit cost	Ingredient cost
Flour	0.300 kg	10 p kg	
Margarine	0.150 kg	60 p kg	
Sugar	0.070 kg	15 p kg	
Eggs	2	4½ p each	
Cooking apples	1¾ kg	30 p kg	
Lemon	1	10 p each	
Granulated sugar	0.200 kg	15 p kg	
Apricot jam	0.200 kg	37 p kg	
		TOTAL	

Yield: 1 Flan of 10 portions
Wastage:
Cost per portion:
Seasonal variation cost:

Fig. 3. Costing sheet for Exercise 35, Question No. 1.

COSTING SHEET

RECIPE   Crème caramel

Ingredient	Quantity	Unit cost	Ingredient cost
Milk	4 litres	12 p litre	
Large eggs	24	6 p each	
Granulated sugar	0.600 kg	15 p kg	
Vanilla stick	2	9 p	
Lump sugar	2 kg	18 p kg	
		TOTAL	

Yield: 40 portions
Wastage:
Cost per portion:
Seasonal variation cost:

Fig. 4. Costing sheet for Exercise 35, Question No. 2.

Menu planning

As previously mentioned, menu planning is also critical for successful food costing. It is the wise manager who knows his clientèle and he will know the prices that his customers will pay for a meal or a dish. There is also a skill in the way Table d'hôte and Banqueting Menus are formulated, so that a more expensive dish with a low profit margin can be included into it because other dishes with a high profit ratio can support the overall selling price to yield an overall gross profit. This is something that is achieved with experience and cannot be taught but each establishment has guide-lines to help formulate all its menu planning. If it doesn't it should think seriously about such a system.

Banquet Menus

If a Banquet Menu has to be costed the same format is followed as that for costing a dish but each course is costed and the adjuncts, i.e. roll and butter, fat needed for frying, paper goods needed for the service or laundering must be included in the overall total, to find the actual cost per portion. Then the gross kitchen percentage needed worked out and then the VAT percentage added.

Example
Find the selling price of the following Banquet Menu and find a selling price to give a 40% kitchen percentage and then the quoted selling price per head to the client.

MENU

Grapefruit	Avocado Cocktail

Filet de sole bercy

Dindonneaux rôtis à l'anglais

Choux de Bruxelles au beurre	Pommes Parisienne

Charlotte russe

Câfé

The ingredients you require are:

Ingredient	Quantity	Unit Cost	Cost £ p	Dish Cost £ p
Grapefruit and Avocado Cocktail				
Mint	Bunch	20 p	20	
Grapefruit	50	10 p each	5.00	
Avocado	30	46 p each	13.80	
Ginger ale	1 litre	46 p litre	46	
Lemons	7	10 p each	70	20.16
Filet de sole bercy				
Lemon sole	25 × ½ kg	£2.40 kg	30.00	
Eggs	12	7 p each	84	
Cream	½ litre	£1.50 litre	75	
Shallots	½ kg	60 p kg	30	
Lemons	2	10 p each	20	
Parsley	Bunch	30 p	30	
White wine	2 bottles	£1.50 each	3.00	
Butter	1 kg	£2.25 kg	2.25	
Margarine	0.100 kg	£1.60 kg	16	
Flour	0.200 kg	30 p kg	6	37.86
Dindonneaux rôtis à l'anglais				
Chipolatas	3 kg	£2.45 kg	7.35	
Turkey	3 × 7 kg	£2.98 kg	62.58	
Watercress	10 bunches	18 p each	1.80	
Brown stock	2 litres	21 p litre	42	
Dripping	¾ kg	50 p kg	38	72.53
Bread Sauce and Stuffing				
Milk	2 litres	50 p litre	1.00	
Eggs	6	7 p each	42	
Onion	1 kg	20 p kg	20	
Lemon	2	10 p each	20	
Thyme	1½ bunches	10 p each	15	
Loaf	4	45 p each	1.80	
Suet	½ kg	56 p kg	28	4.05
Pommes Parisienne				
Potatoes	17 kg	10 p kg	1.70	
Dripping	500 kg	50 p kg	25	
Salt	0.100 kg	30 p	3	1.98
Choux de Bruxelles				
Brussel sprouts	15 kg	36 p kg	5.40	
Butter	1 kg	£2.25 kg	2.25	
Salt	0.050 kg	30 p kg	2	7.67
Charlotte russe				
Milk	4 litres	50 p litre	2.00	
Eggs	35	7 p each	2.45	

Ingredient	Quantity	Unit Cost	Cost £ p	Dish Cost £ p
Single cream	2 litres	£2.25 litre	4.50	
Double cream	2 litres	£3.90 litre	7.80	
Vanilla sticks	2	50 p each	1.00	
Granulated sugar	2 kg	48 p kg	96	
Gelatine sheet	¼ kg	50 p kg	13	18.84
Lady fingers				
Eggs	16	7 p each	1.12	
Caster sugar	½ kg	56 p each	28	
Flour	½ kg	30 p each	15	1.55
Coffee				
Milk	7.5 litres	50 p litre	3.75	
Coffee	1 kg	7.20 kg	7.20	
Demerara sugar	2 kg	.80 p kg	1.60	12.55

TOTAL COST £177.19

Cost per portion $= £\dfrac{177.19}{100}$ (move point 2 places to left)

$= £1.77$ to nearest penny

Additional items optional $=$ 5 Roll and butter

  $\underline{10}$ Paper goods and laundering
  $\underline{£1.92}$

To make a gross profit of 60%

Kitchen percentage $=$ SP − gross profit %
$= 100\% - 60\%$
$= 40\%$

$= \dfrac{\text{Cost price} \times 100}{\text{Kitchen percentage}}$

Therefore apply the formula:

$$\dfrac{192 \times 100}{40}$$

$= £4.80$

Add VAT at 15% $= £4.80$ at 10% $= 48$
$£4.80$ at 5% $= \underline{24}$
$\underline{72}$ p

Selling price + VAT $= £5.52$

EXERCISE 36

Using current price lists and commodity prices cost a Banquet Menu for 100 and find a selling price + VAT to show a gross profit of:

1. 60%   **2.** $66\frac{2}{3}$%   **3.** 70%.

Table d'hôte menus

Sales forecasting here plays an important part because the amount of each dish on the menu that is produced can affect profit margins and customer goodwill. Nothing is more annoying and liable to cause patrons dissatisfaction than a couldn't-care-less attitude and 'it's off'. A good manager will keep a record of actual sales of dishes attached to the menu as a customer's choice is often controlled by the weather, the day and the other dishes available. In establishments with a regular clientèle or captive customer 'menu fatigue' can also affect choice, so that a dish which for weeks has been very popular will suddenly not sell and leave the kitchen with large quantities of a previously popular dish and a shortage of the other items. The costing for the menu is carried out in exactly the same way as for a Banquet Menu, but either the manager or chef must clearly state the kitchen production of each dish. It is when planning these menus that advantage can be taken of the seasonal availability of foods and special offers and so produce interesting and variable menus at advantageous costs.

EXERCISE 37

Using current price lists and commodity prices, indicate production amounts for the kitchen on a Table d'hôte Menu to serve an estimated 100 covers and produce a selling price for the menu to give a 60% gross profit, assuming 100 covers were served. Assume that because of extreme weather conditions only 70 covers were served. What effect would this have on the gross profit for the menu that day?

EXERCISE 38

1. Cost the following Table d'hôte Menu using the given recipes and a current price list.

2. Produce a selling price for the menu overleaf assuming that our restaurant works on a 60% gross profit percentage.

MENU

Grapefruit and Orange Cocktail
Fresh Cream of Mushroom Soup
Spaghetti Napolitaine

******

Roast Leg of English Lamb — Mint Sauce
Cheese Omelette
Fried Fillet of Plaice

******

Buttered Garden Peas
French Fried Potatoes
Roast Potatoes

******

Lemon Pancakes
Fresh Pineapple Flambée
Mushrooms on Toast

******

Coffee

RECIPES

Mushroom Soup (4 portions)
50 g butter
1 litre white stock
100 g onion, leek, celery

125 ml milk

50 g flour
100 g mushrooms
Bouquet garni seasoning

Spaghetti Napolitaine (4 portions)
100 g spaghetti
25 g grated cheese
25 g butter

½ pt tomato sauce

100 g tomato concassée
10 g chopped onion
100 g tomatoes

Lemon Pancakes (4 portions)
100 g flour
1 egg
25 g caster sugar
1 lemon

EXERCISE 39

Produce a selling price for the menu below using your own recipes and assuming that you are working with a kitchen percentage of 40% state whether or not you have included VAT. (Use current prices.)

TABLE D'HÔTE LUNCHEON

Cream of Tomato Soup
Chilled Grapefruit Cocktail

* * * * * *

Spaghetti with Meat and Tomato Sauce
Baked Egg in Cream

* * * * * *

Grilled Fillets of Lemon Sole with Shrimp Butter

* * * * * *

Brown Lamb Stew with Vegetable Garnish
Chicken in White Wine Sauce
Grilled Pork Chop with Apple

* * * * * *

Creamed Potatoes
Chipped Potatoes
Mixed Dice of Vegetables
Braised Celery

* * * * * *

Cold cuts of Ham, Beef, Turkey with Salad

* * * * * *

Baked Pineapple Upside-down Pudding and Custard
Treacle Tart and Cream
Cheese and Biscuits

* * * * * *

Coffee

Monthly figures for food cost and gross profit

Once we have carefully calculated the costings for dishes to be sold and banquets given, it remains to be seen whether actual operations over a period of time have come up to expectations.

The food cost is taken away from the takings for a month, and what is left is gross profit. This can be expressed as a percentage of takings. We will already know roughly what we expect this percentage to be in order to cover other expenses and net profit, and will have based our dish costing on it.

The calculation of the food cost for the month will not, however, be arrived at in the same way as for a dish — it is not possible in a restaurant to list the ingredients of all the meals prepared in a month. The total is determined by reference to the total value of food purchased in the month and by finding out how much of this we have used. This can be done by deducting what is left at the end of the month from the total amount of food we have had during the month. The amount left at the end of the month is known as *closing stock* and will start us off for the next month's sales when it will be known as *opening stock*. The closing stock of one month is the opening stock of the next month.

Having added all our purchases of food for the month, we add the total to the value of opening stock, and from this total deduct the closing stock. The result is the cost of the food.

Food cost = Opening stock + Purchases − Closing stock

Example

The net purchases of food during the month of June amounted to £875, the value of stock on June 1st being £115, and on June 30th, £168. What was the cost of food consumed during the month?

Answer:

	£
Opening stock	115
Purchases	875
	990
Less closing stock	168
Cost of food consumed	£ 822

The total of the purchases should be *net* after deducting any returns or allowances. This should be borne in mind particularly when goods have been returned just before the end of the month, and a credit note has not been received.

The calculation of the *food percentage* is as follows:

Example

Cost of food consumed during the month = £822.

Sales resulting from food consumed during the month = £2154.

$$\text{Food percentage} = \frac{\text{Food cost} \times 100}{\text{Food takings}}$$

$$= \frac{822 \times 100}{2154} = \frac{82200}{2154} = 38.16\%$$

5
Recipes and Kitchen Operations

Introduction

A recipe is obviously a list of ingredients and instructions for their preparation to produce a dish. Yet such information can be given to twenty people and the end-products be so variable that one might justifiably query whether the recipe had been followed or whether indeed it was reliable.

But do we want such a situation that every Coq au vin the world over tastes exactly the same? What would be the point of eating in different restaurants if the chef's individual flair and expertise were not allowed full rein?

Recipes

What is the point of a recipe and how important is it? Some of the most popular and tasty dishes can never be created again because they were the result of using the commodities available in the kitchen at the time in unspecified amounts, or as a result of some adaptation to the recipe because of a mistake or lack of ingredient. This can happen in spite of carefully recording the amounts of the commodities used to produce the dish. From a business and profitability point of view there is much truth in the old adage that the clever cook is the one who can produce something out of nothing.

However, most cooking needs to follow a systematic plan. Since Apicius, exponents of cookery have written down the ingredients and method of preparation. Had they not done so, we should be in a sad plight indeed. They have carefully recorded their culinary wisdom and skill so that their methods and dishes can be reproduced or interpreted as we see fit. Dishes are handed down through families, communities leave their countries and live in other parts of the world and take their culinary skills with them, and shortages of commodities occur causing improvisations that produce new combinations and repasts for the daily diet. All of these have resulted in some form of recording which has produced countless number of recipe and cookery books available for use. It is up to the establishment to decide what use is to be made of a recipe and how slavishly it is to be followed.

With the development of convenience products, fast-food operations and franchised outlets, the public expect that when they buy a Kentucky Fried Chicken or a tin of Heinz Tomato Soup a certain recognisable flavour which they like will be present. This has meant that the large-scale food manufacturers produce a standardised recipe for every one of their products so that whenever it is made it will always be the same. If this policy was followed in a smaller establishment with a regular clientèle, the customers would soon find other eating-houses, since they would become bored with the dishes. One organisation has tried to have the best of both worlds and puts variations into a standard recipe like this:

Week 1 Steak and Kidney Pie + Worcestershire Sauce

Week 2 Steak and Kidney Pie + Mushroom Essence

Week 3 Steak and Kidney Pie + Chopped Parsley

Week 4 Steak and Kidney Pie + Ground Pepper

As will be shown in later chapters of the book, in order to produce satisfactory profit margins some control has to be exerted on the purchasing and use of commodities. The first stages in this control are to be found in the recipe. A good recipe will state:

1. Quantity
2. Commodity
3. Method of production
4. Yield.

The identification of the commodity is particularly vital because when foodstuffs are ordered it is important that the right items are purchased. In larger establishments the buying department will have produced a quality control guide for their suppliers. This will establish, for example, when Sirloin Steak is ordered, that the steak supplied must be within a given weight range (sometimes known as 'purchasing tolerance') trimmed, have a certain percentage relationship of fat and meat, and be either English or imported meat. The storeman may even have an identical photograph to the supplier showing the accepted standard of product so that he can check the quality on arrival at the establishment.

The method of production and yield are both important, because if the product is overcooked the number of portions that can be served from it will be reduced, as will the profitability of the dish.

Adapting recipes to the number of portions required

If a recipe is selected that is geared to produce four portions, and 100 portions are required, then the recipe quantities given must be increased proportionately. This is done in the following way.

(i)   Find out how many portions a recipe should produce.

(ii)   To produce a given number of portions, find a figure that when multiplied by the basic recipe portions will yield the right amount.

For example, if a recipe for 25 is needed to yield 100 portions, multiply by $\frac{100}{25} = 4$,

or if a recipe produces 10 portions and you need 100, multiply by 10. When you have found the multiple you multiply the ingredient list quantities by it.

Example

A recipe for 4 portions of Navarin of Lamb is needed to produce 100 portions. Find the quantities needed.

Navarin of Lamb

Ingredient	Quantity for 4 portions	× 2½ = Quantity for 10 portions	× 10 = Quantity for 100 portions
Stewing lamb	500 g	1.25 kg	12.50 kg
Plain flour	25 g	62.5 g	625 g
Brown stock	500 ml	1 ½ litres	2 ½ litres
Spanish onion	100 g	250 g	2.5 kg
Dripping	25 g	$62\frac{1}{2}$ g	625 g
Tomato pureé	10 g	25 g	250 g
Carrot	100 g	250 g	2.5 kg
Salt	5	12.5 g	*
Pepper	2 g	5 g	*
Clove of garlic	1	1 large	*
Bouquet garni	1	1 large	*

* When multiplying up recipes seasonings should not be doubled up in the same way. For example, 10 Bouquet garni would not be added but one large one. Philéas Gilbert in the 1931 edition of *La Cuisine de Tous les Mois* defines a pinch of salt as 7.8 grams and a turn of the peppermill as 2 grams. This is usually overcome by stating 'seasoning to taste' but when costing a recipe even the amount of salt and pepper used has to be accounted for.

EXERCISE 40

Use your own recipe book.

1. Find the quantities required to produce 100 portions of:

    (a) Cream of Mushroom Soup   (b) Chicken fricassée

2. Find the quantities required for:

    (a) 10 Apple Flans   (b) 25 Swiss Rolls

3. Find the quantities required to produce 10 portions from a 100-portion recipe.

Weight loss

During bad storage evaporation of moisture can occur which will reduce the purchased weight but more noticeable are the weight losses which occur during preparation, cooking and service.

Allowing for weight loss in preparation

Unless products are purchased ready-prepared and portioned, there will inevitably be weight loss as a result of storage (maybe) and preparation (definitely). This loss must be allowed for and included in the calculations when establishing the selling

71

price of a dish. The main commodities which show weight loss during preparation are meat, fish, poultry, vegetables and fruit. There are generally accepted percentages allowed for preparation loss. For example, 50% wastage is tolerable for the preparation of fillets from a whole plaice, but it is not only prudent but good housekeeping to keep a check on your own establishment's percentage weight loss during preparation. This is done by weighing the product on arrival in the kitchen, preparing it and weighing the non-saleable remains.

Example

Shoulder of Lamb delivered at 32 kg (15 shoulders)

After preparing ready for oven weight 27 kg

Therefore preparation loss = 32 − 27 = 5 kg

Therefore percentage loss $= \dfrac{5}{32} \times \dfrac{100}{1}$ %

$$= 15.6\%$$

It is important to remember that when costing a dish you use the cost of *saleable* meat not the *purchase* price of the meat. The meat above was delivered at £1.10 per kg. Therefore, it cost £35.20 but the meat available to be cooked was only 27 kg so the cost per kg is now

$$£\dfrac{35.20}{27} = £1.30\,p$$

When preparing standard ordering levels it is sensible to note the acceptable percentage waste loss and make spot checks upon this.

Another aspect of weight loss which is often forgotten can occur if the supplier does not send the actual weight ordered but sends more. If the kitchen staff notice this and only cook the amount specified on the standard recipe, all will be well, but if 15 kg of diced chuck steak was ordered and 15 ½ kg sent and cooked as the required amount, the cost of the meat item will be in excess of the standard planned for. Thus it is vital that when goods are ordered only the actual amount required as estimated on the sales forecast should be stated.

Example

Sales forecast   150 portions of dish

                           20 portions for staff

Total planned production 170

Ordering standard 12 ½ kg per 100 portions

$$
\begin{aligned}
\text{Therefore correct ordering amount} = 100 \text{ portions} &= 12\frac{1}{2} \text{ kg} \\
50 \text{ portions} &= 6\frac{1}{4} \text{ kg} \\
10 \text{ portions} &= 1\frac{1}{4} \text{ kg} \\
10 \text{ portions} &= 1\frac{1}{4} \text{ kg} \\
&= 21\frac{1}{2} \text{ kg}
\end{aligned}
$$

Actual amount ordered = 22 kg

The extra $\frac{3}{4}$ kg should be used profitably if possible. If it is wasted, the profit margin will suffer.

Allowing for weight loss in cooking

When food is cooked, particularly by boiling, roasting, baking and grilling, moisture is driven off which will cause a reduction in the weight of the product to be served. For example, a joint of pork can enter the oven at 11 kg, and when the approved cooking methods (as stated in standard recipe) are followed, its cooked weight should be 8 kg, but if overcooked the final weight might be $7\frac{1}{4}$ kg.

This means that if the cooked weight portion size is 50 g then $\frac{750}{50} = 15$ portions have been lost and no income can be received for them.

Another cause for losing portions is the incomplete transfer of ingredients from one container to another. If a container is not scraped down properly in a large production run, two or three portions can be lost.

Fig. 5 represents four days of a Kitchen Production Sheet which would be filled in daily. The chef or manager would indicate the number of portions required for the menu and then the production numbers and sold figures are filled in. It is essential that these are looked at regularly, and if there is an under-production against certain dishes, questions should be asked and the standard recipe and method checked. Any form of record keeping is only as good as the use to which you put it.

Monday	Number produced	Number sold	Tuesday	Number produced	Number sold
Assorted Chilled Fruit Juices	10	10	Assorted Chilled Fruit Juices	8	8
Grapefruit Segments	5	5	Macaroni Cheese	12	8
Cream of Tomato Soup	20	18	Consommé	20	20
Roast Beef with Yorkshire Pudding	50	50	Stuffed Roast Shoulder of Lamb	48	40
Cheese & Onion Pie	24	20	Lancashire Hot Pot	30	29
Scotch Egg	18	12	Grilled Pork Sausage	12	8
Salmon Salad	6	6	Grosvenor Pie Salad	5	5
Roast Potatoes	50	48	Croquette Potatoes	50	50
Chipped Potatoes	50	50	Lyonnaise Potatoes	50	50
Buttered Carrots	40	35	Garden Peas	40	40
Broad Beans	40	20	Braised Leeks	30	28
Rice Pudding	18	12	Pineapple Fritters & Syrup Sauce	24	24
Gooseberry Pie & Custard	30	28	Chocolate Sponge & Custard	24	20
Lemon Mousse	15	15	Fruit Trifle	20	18
Cheese & Biscuits	5	5	Cheese & Biscuits	6	6

Fig. 5 Food production sales chart analysis

Wednesday	Number produced	Number sold	Thursday	Number produced	Number sold
Assorted Chilled Fruit Juices	8		Assorted Chilled Fruit Juices	8	
Chilled Honeydew Melon	12		Liver Sausage with Salad	10	
Cream of Celery Soup	20		Minestrone	20	
Roast Pork with Stuffing & Apple Sauce	55		Roast Chicken with Bread Sauce	55	
Chicken Curry with Savoury Rice	20		Grilled Liver and Bacon	20	
Steak & Kidney Pudding	12		Fish Cakes	10	
Corned Beef Salad	5		Cheddar Cheese Salad	5	
Roast Potatoes	50		Duchesse Potatoes	50	
Chipped Potatoes	50		Sauté Potatoes	50	
Kidney Beans	40		Baked Beans	40	
Cauliflower with Cheese	30		Sweet Corn	40	
Semolina & Jam Sauce	18		Baked Egg Custard	24	
Rhubarb Crumble & Custard	24		Dutch Apple Pie & Custard	24	
Peach Flan	20		Pear Melba	20	
Cheese & Biscuits	5		Cheese & Biscuits	5	

Comments

1. Roast Beef to be increased as sold out during second sitting.
2. Overproduced Scotch Eggs and Broad Beans.
3. Must increase Lemon Mousse — very popular with customers.
4. Macaroni not popular, reduce numbers next time.
5. Reduce Lamb by 2 lb when next ordered.
6. Increase Pineapple Fritters.

EXERCISE 41

1. Complete the following chart to show percentage weight loss during preparation. (Any other items you are using can be calculated.)

Item	Purchased weight	Prepared weight	% Weight loss
Potatoes, old			
Potatoes, new			
1 whole plaice, filleted			
Undressed chicken			

2. Complete the following chart for the listed items (or any other product you are using) to show percentage weight loss during cooking.

Item	Purchased weight	Prepared weight	Percentage weight loss	Cooked weight	% weight loss through cooking
Leg of pork					
Lemon sole					
Best end of lamb					
Potatoes as chips					

3. Find the new cost per 100 gram when using kitchen-prepared goods.

Item	Purchased weight	Unit cost	Prepared weight	New unit cost
Brussel sprouts	1 kg			
Shin of beef	1000 g			
Ox kidney	500 g			
Onions				
Lettuce				

Portion loss

The main reasons for this loss is that either the kitchen or service staff have not been trained to give the correct portions for each dish or that the management have not provided the right equipment, containers or dishes for the food service. Another cause of loss is the human element: service staff may have favourite customers! It is the kitchen's responsibility to portion the food and/or tell the service staff how many portions they are to get from any given item.

Loss prevention

It doesn't matter how many control systems are put in if good supervision and spot-checks are not instigated. Management policy should be to carry out regular investigations into all the aspects of ordering, buying, storage, production, cooking and service of food, not forgetting regular checking of refrigerators and the use of left-over foods. The efficient establishment is the one where staff are kept constantly on their toes and where they are encouraged to meet targets and are rewarded for so doing. Incentive schemes and interdepartmental competitions can aid this.

As the losses mentioned in this chapter can be financially disastrous if not checked at an early stage, it is worth listing them again:

(i)   Bad menu planning.

(ii)   Inaccurate sales forecasting.

(iii)   Poor purchasing.

(iv)   Inaccurate ordering or poor checking on delivery.

(v)   No reference being made to standard recipes and yields.

(vi)   Poor preparation of commodities.

(vii)   Over or undercooking of food.

(viii) Poor portion control.

(ix)   Little or no use being made of left-over foods.

(x)   Theft or 'picking'.

It is important to remember that even if establishments have chosen to obtain as many items as possible pre-portioned, this in itself does not stop losses as many people have found ways of working a fiddle to overcome this.

EXERCISE 42

Using the points (i) — (x) above:

1.   Explain what is meant by them.

2.   State how they can be checked.

3.   Give the possible results if they occur.

4.   Suggest ways of remedying them.

5.   In whose job descriptions would you incorporate different aspects of loss prevention?

6.   What training would you include in staff induction to ensure an understanding of these points?

7.   As a manager what spot checks would you carry out and how often?

6
Food Control

Introduction

In catering, the cost of the materials used is very great. A medium-sized hotel, for example, will carry somewhere in the region of £5000 worth of beverage stock alone. Money tied up, for that is what it is, is a costly business — bear in mind that during 1987 money could be invested very simply and produce at least 10% interest. If the business is having to borrow money to purchase stock, then the effect is even greater, and if follows, therefore, that efficient control of stock levels will improve the profitability of the business.

The problems and difficulties of controlling food

The principal difficulties of controlling food are as follows.

(i)   Food prices fluctuate frequently, for many reasons:

    (a)   inflation,

    (b)   falls in demand or supply (usually because of poor harvests, e.g. potatoes after the 1976 drought, coffee after the frost in South America in 1976),

    (c)   EEC Regulations — removal of food subsidies in recent years from the UK to produce compatibility with our European neighbours,

    (d)   increased transport costs — increased wage costs to haulage companies and increased fuel costs following the oil price rises starting, particularly, in 1973—74,

    (e)   changes in customer demand altering the cost of food by either producing a glut (when demand falls) or a scarcity (when demand increases). In recent years we have even seen prices rise because of the public creating a false shortage by hoarding. Sugar and salt are perhaps the best examples and one can imagine the effect on the placing of a cruet on a guest's table! Advertising, both within the establishment or nationally, may increase demand, whilst changes in taste may move the demand from one product to another. Demand for a product may also change because of the following considerations:

(1)   health (is the comsumption of too much sugar going to cause cancer?, does salt harden the arteries?, do dairy products produce heart disease?),

(2)   moral (should we kill animals for food?, should we eat eggs from battery hens?),

(3)   financial (can I afford to buy meat?).

(ii)   Catering food stocks are bought and sold, with luck, quickly. Food is perishable and, therefore, should be purchased, cooked and consumed in as short a time as possible. Delay may cause:

(a)   deterioration in taste,

(b)   deterioration in colour, texture or appearance,

(c)   possible build up of bacteria, creating a health risk.

(iii)   Most catering establishments require a wide variety of different food items. The more items there are to look after the more problems there will be implementing control. Consider, for example, the number of herbs and spices required to operate a hotel kitchen.

Factors affecting control systems

There is *no* standard control system for catering, and as in book-keeping, the system should be adaptable and suit the individual needs of the establishment.

The factors present, in catering, which result in a very *complex* control system are:

(i)   There being regular changes of the entire menu.

(ii)   A menu, either à la carte or table d'hôte, containing a large number of dishes.

(iii)   Menu dishes having a large number of ingredients.

(iv)   Individual dishes requiring lengthy cooking times.

(v)   The presence of restaurant carved or prepared dishes, e.g. ribs of beef.

(vi)   The sweet trolley.

The presence of one or more of the above items will produce problems of control because:

(i)   There is a problem of forecasting customer demand.

(ii)   Losses will occur with overcooking.

(iii) More storage space is required to keep the 'back up' stock in, because more food items will be required.

(iv)   There is more chance of food being 'left over', resulting in loss. One hotel manager states that, on a quiet day, he can lose up to £20 worth of food from his sweet trolley alone!

It follows, therefore, that a control system can be made more simple when the following form an integral part of the operation:

(i)   The menu remains the same from day to day.

(ii)   The menu has a strictly limited number of dishes, which are of the 'unit' type — e.g. pre-portioned steak, whole trout, dover sole, lamb cutlets, pork chops, etc. As an alternative, convenience foods have the same effect — e.g. boil-in-the-bag products. (What about the cost to the customer though?)

(iii) The menu is of the 'call-order' type — i.e. the cooking of the dish does not commence until the dish is ordered by the customer.

The advantages of the above points are that food items, kept in stock, will not vary, except in quantity. Forecasting demand is easier, stocktaking is easier, and costing is more accurate.

There are many examples of national companies which have adopted the above principles with considerable success — e.g. Berni Inns, Trophy Taverns, etc.

In *any establishment*, if control is to be effective, the following points must be noted:

(i)   Food stocks must be secure — that is, locked up when not being requisitioned, with a responsible person in charge. Refrigerators, deep-freezers and kitchens must also be locked when not in use.

(ii)   An accounting or book-keeping system must be present, which will monitor the results of the operation daily.

(iii) The production of food over the hotplate must be controlled by a responsible person to ensure accurate portion control, appearance, temperature, etc. If the restaurant is responsible for portion control (e.g. the carving trolley, the sweet trolley, etc.), then communication between the kitchen and restaurant staff is *essential*. The restaurant *must* be told the portion requirement and their results *must* be checked.

Management, in the smaller establishment, or the Control Office, in the larger, should make daily checks and spot checks on the efficiency of the above points.

It must be appreciated, that if any of the above factors are either omitted or not functioning correctly, then the whole control system will have failed.

Food, before it reaches the customer, is processed in some way. During the process the cost will rise. In order to keep this rise to a minimum, and therefore either produce more profit or reduce the selling price, each stage must be carefully controlled. The usual methods of monitoring the food processing are:

(i)   Weighing – before and after cooking.

(ii)   Expert cooking.

(iii)   Recording the actual portions produced, and sold.

(iv)   Recycling unused food – either resulting from preparation, or unsold food.

(v)   Waste control – portion control techniques?

Before the food can be processed it must be bought. Consideration must be given to buying a *consistent* product at a *consistent* price. (Should we always buy the best?) Failure will result in repeated costing exercises or lost profit. In order that management may compare price quotations from their suppliers, accurate purchase specifications must be produced. For example:

    Lamb (whole)
    Welsh, spring
    Delivered in two halves
    Including kidneys

Quotations should be obtained from at least two suppliers. The order would then be placed with the supplier who satisfies the majority of the following criteria:

Price

Quality

Reliability

Note, when considering price, that care should be taken to ensure that any discount offered is genuine, so on the arrival of the goods:

(i)   The quality should be checked — is it what was ordered?

(ii)   The price should be checked — invoice price with quoted price.

(iii)   The quantity should be checked — that is, when receiving meat, weigh it and check with the delivery note and the invoice.

Discounts have been mentioned earlier, but since they are a common feature of commercial life, they bear further explanation. It is now quite common for suppliers to offer discount for large purchases in the form of a reduced basic price. For example: a wine merchant may offer to supply Beaujolais to you for £3.00 per bottle (assuming you just want one bottle) or at £33.00 per case, if you are prepared to buy 12 bottles. It can be seen that to buy at £33.00 per case as opposed to £3.00 per bottle represents a saving of £3.00 for every 12 purchased! Perhaps the idea all started with the baker's dozen?

The price per case may then be further reduced if the caterer decides to buy several cases. In the same example, the wine merchant may offer Beaujolais to you at £33.00 per case for the first four cases but then say to you; 'If you purchase six cases we will let you have them at £30.00 per case.' His price list may, therefore, look something like this:

	Btl.	1 – 4 cases	5 – 10 cases	11 – 20 cases	21 + cases
Beaujolais	£3.00	£33.00	£30.00	£27.00	£25.00

The different prices would be for *full* cases only, so that if the caterer ordered 124 bottles, it would all be supplied at £30.00 per case of 12 and the total cost would be £310.00.

The caterer must decide at which case rate to buy at according to his needs. It would be pointless purchasing 21 cases of Beaujolais if it would take him three years to sell the wine! The saving he makes by buying such a lot would be more than offset by the money he could make b, purchasing say one case and investing the rest of the money in the bank for three years.

It is, perhaps, the area of banqueting which provides the most scope for savings of this nature.

Documentation

Many of the smaller establishments will place their orders with their suppliers by telephone, and some of the larger catering suppliers now operate a 'tele sale' operation where the supplier will telephone the catering establishment at a pre-arranged time. The advantage of this system is that it cuts down the paper work, and, with a bit of luck, speeds up the service to the caterer. It will also compensate for the caterer who forgets to make an order! Care should be taken, however, to ensure that you do not fall into the trap of saying 'now that they are on the phone, I may as well order something'.

The larger establishment will probably operate within formal specifications and documentation. Any *order* made by the establishment should be signed by a person in authority with additional copies being made for the person receiving the goods, the storeman, perhaps; and for retention in the records.

ORDER			
From: Ivor Business, Sometown To: Catersupply Anytown Please supply:	No: 098078 Ref: I/B Date: 12/11/81		
Quantity	Pk	Description	Unit price
1 case 3 cases	A10 A2½	Pear halves Fruit cocktail	£12.40 £ 3.85
Signed:		Hotel Manager.	

It should be remembered that the person placing the order should take account of best buying rates. Many companies will offer goods at a reduced price if bought by the case or multiple cases. However, it is bad policy simply to order large quantities to obtain discount if the goods are going to remain in stock for long periods of time.

Before ordering, take into account:

(i)   What is required, in the short term, by the department requiring the goods.

(ii)   How much you already have in stock, and what physical space is available.

(iii) The shelf life or perishability of the product.

(iv)   The frequency of delivery.

(v)   The minimum quantity that can be delivered.

(vi)   The cost of providing the finance and/or inflation rates?

(vii) Whether the commodity is going to appreciate in the near future.

When the goods are delivered they should be accompanied by a *delivery note*. (For alcoholic goods this is a legal requirement!) The delivery note will make the caterer aware of any changes in quality, quantity or pack size at the time of delivery and, on receipt of the caterer's signature, authorise the supplier to demand payment.

Name and address Ivor Business, Sometown	*Delivery instructions* Deliver after 11.00 a.m. Collect empty cases.		*Delivery note* Catersupply Anytown No. 7867897 Date: 20/11/8
Quantity	*Size*	*Item*	*Code*
6 36	A10 A2½	Pear halves Fruit cocktail	0989 0954
Received in good condition			

Within the establishment the staff will 'marry up' the delivery note with the order form (if there is one) and await the receipt of the *invoice* from the supplier.

		INVOICE			
		Catersupply			
Tel. 000 1188		Anytown		VAT No. 000 1111 00	
Invoice No. 2345 to:					
		Ivor Business, Sometown.			
Qty	*Unit*	*Description*	*Price per*	*£ p*	*VAT Code*
6	A10	Pear halves	24.80 doz	12.40	01
36	A2½	Fruit cocktail	3.85 doz	11.55	01
			TOTAL:	23.95	

Following the receipt of the invoice(s), or usually within one month, the supplier will issue a *statement of account*. Any invoices received will be checked, firstly against the delivery note to see that the goods being charged for were, in fact, delivered; and secondly against the price list or quotation to ensure that the correct price has been charged and any discounts offered have been included.

		STATEMENT			
		Catersupply			
Ivor Business, Sometown.		Anytown	Date: 31/12/81		
Date	*Our ref*	*Trans*	*Debit*	*Credit*	*Balance*
	Bal/Fwd		45.97		45.97
4 DEC	DECEMBER	CASH		45.97	00.00
20 DEC	2345	INV	23.95		23.95

All invoices will now be checked off against the statement to ensure that all have been recorded correctly. Any goods which have been returned to the supplier, perhaps because they were of the wrong quality or damaged, will be recorded by the supplier on a *credit note*. These are usually printed in red and would be included on the statement as if the supplier had received payment.

Many of the larger establishments will also record the receipt of goods in a *goods received book* to form a more permanent record. Containers on which deposits have been charged would also be noted in this book. This is particularly important with respect to alcoholic beverages since, in these days, the deposit on the container and case is often more than the cost of the product!

The life of perishable goods may be extended if consideration is given to the maintenance of correct: *temperature* at which they are stored; *humidity* and *ventilation* of the store; and *stock rotation*.

Stock control of dry stores

The most common system of dry goods control is the *bin card* system. Each product is allocated a card on which is recorded the date, quantity of product received, quantity issued and the balance remaining. In addition, the card may contain information about:

(i)   The normal supplier (address and telephone number).

(ii)   The minimum order that can be placed.

(iii)   The order day/delivery day.

(iv)   The wholesale price — after allowing any discount.

These bin cards would be maintained by the storekeeper, who would up-date the information on the card. He would also be responsible for issuing the old stock first. Spot checks should be made, by management, to ensure accuracy, and the balance figures for each card would be used for stocktaking purposes at the end of each accountancy period.

An example of a bin card for A10 Fruit Cocktail would be:

Item: FRUIT COCKTAIL Quality: S.A.			Pack: A2½ Price: 32 p.		
Date	*Reference*	*In*	*Out*	*Balance*
14 Nov.	Balance B/Fwd			5
20 Dec.	*Catersupply*	36		41
23 Dec.	Kitchen		6	35
Supplier: Catersupply Anytown (000 1188) Order: Mon. Del. up Fri.					

In normal practice the storekeeper would issue goods at pre-set times during the day. Issues would be backed by a requisition from the appropriate departments, which has been signed, as authorisation, by either management or designated responsible person (Head Chef, Head Barman, Head Housekeeper, etc.).

Food on arrival going straight to the kitchen (e.g. fresh fish and meat) would be charged to the kitchen on receipt of goods and delivery note.

It is essential to know what the value of food sold in any particular accounting period is. This value is found by 'taking stock' and valuing the stock remaining, or closing stock, at cost price. Where stocks have differing values, because they have either been bought at different times or from different suppliers, then the method of valuation may take the form of an average price, a separate price for each commodity or the current buying price. The latter is often considered to be the best method since catering establishments tend to work on high stock turnover, and prices in recent years have tended to always rise. Any price rise should be communicated to management so that alterations to costings of dishes can be made.

At the end of an accounting period, very often one month, the cost of food used is calculated by inserting figures into the following equation:

(Opening stock + Purchases) − Closing stock = Cost of food used

Example
Opening stock: £764.00   Purchases: £2574.00   Closing stock: £827.00.

Therefore:

$$\text{Cost of food used} = (764 + 2574) - 827$$
$$= 3338 - 827$$
$$= £2511$$

The cost of food *used* may not always be the cost of food *sold* since some food may have been used to feed the staff, or given away to irate customers who have complained! Some food, in the form of oranges, lemons, eggs, etc., may also have been issued to the bars. Some may also have been stolen, although, in theory, you will not be aware of this value!

An allowance can be made for the above, with the exception of stolen food, against the cost of food used, to produce a cost-of-food-sold figure. The wages account would then be charged for staff meals, the bar for its food and any food given away written off as an expense.

Taking the same example, we may get:

		£
Cost of food used:		2511
Less: Staff meals	256	
Bar food	21	
Gifts	15	
	292	292
Cost of food sold		2219

It is this figure which we would then compare with sales, or takings, to establish the gross profit made. Remember, the *gross* profit is the trading profit, or the difference between sales and the cost of those sales.

Say the sales for the period were £5372; then the gross profit would be calculated as follows:

	£	
Sales	5372	(100%)
Less cost of food sold	2219	(41.3%)
Gross profit	3153	(58.7%)

Sales, as we have shown in Chapter 4, are always regarded as being 100% of business, and it can, therefore, be seen that the gross profit represents 58.7% of the sales figure. The cost of food sold figure must, therefore, be 100% less 58.7%, i.e. 41.3%, and (as we know already) this percentage is usually refered to as the kitchen percentage or the food cost percentage.

If the target percentage gross profit, in the above example, was 60% (a common feature in today's catering) then, on this occasion, there is a shortfall of 1.3% or £69.83. Although percentages are still in common use today when budgeting gross profits and costing dishes, maybe, in the future, there will be a trend towards operating on a 'cost-plus' basis; but that is another subject.

Food stocks, and the compilation of gross profit, may be calculated at the end of pre-set periods of time – weekly, monthly, quarterly or even every year. However, it is often necessary to establish how the business is progressing on a day-to-day basis. In order to do this, food consumption is *estimated* by adding the stores issues to any direct kitchen charges (food issued directly to the kitchen). It must be remembered that this system will take no account of any food stocks remaining in the kitchen, and is, therefore, only to be used as a *guide* to what is going on. Estimation of food consumption and its comparison with sales or takings will provide a good indication as to the progress of the business, and, perhaps, provide a warning system when things begin to go wrong. Accurate stocktaking will then prove the figures one way or the other.

Portion control standards

In order that the correct or budgeted profit is produced, the kitchen must adhere to the concepts of using:

Standard recipes
Standard portions

The correct ingredients must have been originally purchased, otherwise the recipe will be wrong and possibly the yield produced (number of portions) altered if the same portion size is kept.

Standard recipes

A standard recipe will specify the final product and the method of production.

Some establishments (Wimpy Bars, for example) may even supply pictures or photographs, showing exactly how the final product should look; thus being of benefit to both the staff and the customer. It is very important, should pictures be used, that the final product does, in fact, resemble the picture — one can imagine the restaurant full of guests all comparing their plate of food with the picture on the wall, with much mutterings. Remember, also, the Trade Descriptions Act.

The recipe should also indicate the correct yield, or number of portions to be produced from a given quantity of food. Remember that this yield will alter if the method of production is altered. Note especially that the following will always reduce the yield:

(i)   Bad, or wasteful preparation.

(ii)   Overcooking (i.e. cooking for too long).

(iii)   Cooking at excessive temperature.

Standard portions

Having determined the optimum portion size, then management will:

(i)   instruct the staff concerned,

(ii)   provide the correct equipment.

Examples of portion control equipment would be: ladles of known capacity, dough dividers, scoops of known size, regulated slicing machines and, for those who have heard of 'the Fiddler's elbow', sharp knives!

The kitchen *must* inform the restaurant staff of the portion requirements. For example if, Ribs of Beef are to be carved in the restaurant, the staff must be told the portion size and the number of portions to be produced from the rib, and their results must be checked — periodic checks must be made to check the operation and the results *must be controlled*.

Forecasting sales

In order that accurate purchasing can take place, it is necessary to forecast sales by predicting customer choice and volume of demand. This is very often a 'sixth sense' that the caterer develops over a period of time. The yardstick is not to try to educate the public into eating just the dishes you are prepared to prepare, but to find out what the public would like to eat and then go out and sell it. There is some information which the astute caterer will find of use when it comes to predicting customer demand, and it falls into three principal areas, so the caterer should:

(i)   Keep a record of the numbers of each dish sold from a menu.

(ii)   Find out the average spending by customers, taking care to remove the beverage or other spending by the customer.

(iii)   Calculate the proportion, usually expressed as a percentage, of each dish sold, in relation to total sales — does the sale of Fillet Steak represent 50% of the total sales?

There is, of course, a fourth area for consideration, and that is our old friend *common sense*. Technically it is called *catering for the circumstance* and it simply means 'putting the correct dishes on the menu according to the type of clientèle who normally dine there'.

For example, consider a staff canteen serving 500+ meals a day. The catering manager has to decide which of the following menus to put on sale for luncheon on a Tuesday:

Menu A	*Menu B*	*Menu C*
Tripe and Onions	Roast Lamb	Minute Steaks
or	or	or
Roast Lamb	Roast Chicken	Stuffed Ox Heart

If either Menu A or Menu C were to be put on, it would be a fair bet that there would be very little sale of either the Tripe and Onions or the Ox Heart. The above menus are based on the fact that they would all be the same price, because of subsidy, perhaps; but the same rule would apply if the Catering Manager decided to 'educate' his factory workers into eating Smoked Salmon at around £6.50 a portion.

Prevention of loss

Loss of profit can arise for the following reasons.

(i) Meat is used for a purpose for which it was not intended (e.g. using fillet steak for the production of beefburgers).

(ii) Ordering commodities is done entirely on the basis of what can be produced, without considering customer demand, or without any thought to production standards (or, for that matter, what the staff are capable of preparing).

(iii) Poor trimming, butchery or peeling take place. For example, 100×8 oz steaks cut at 8.2 oz will result in a loss of 20 oz or the revenue from 2½ steaks.

(iv) There is bad cooking — overcooking will result in shrinkage or food which cannot be sold; undercooking will result in possibly inedible or returned food.

(v) Portion sizes are not adhered to — remember the sweet trolley and the possibility of restaurant staff giving too much, extra portions, more cream, and so on. The waiter may well think that the young lady smiling up at him is the best thing since the silicon chip, but he is costing the business money!

(vi) Members of the staff are stealing. Good control will usually indicate theft, particularly on the food side, but remember, the beverage side is wide open to the possibility of undetectable theft. Bear in mind, as well, that the most common theft from a kitchen is that of the staff eating the products. It is not a bad idea to insist that all kitchen and restaurant staff have their meal *before* service. There is nothing which dulls the appetite more than a full stomach.

EXERCISE 43

1. Write a short essay (of perhaps not more than one page) on one of the following subjects:

   (a) What are the principal problems of controlling food within an establishment you are familiar with?

   (b) What trends do you foresee customers making in the next decade?

   (c) What are the main problems to operating a menu consisting of only convenience foods?

   (d) What techniques would you adopt when trying to forecast customer demand?

2. A supplier is offering you a cash discount of 5% based on the following price list:

	2 cases	4 cases	6 cases	8 cases
A2½ Fruit Cocktail (12)	3.60	3.30	3.05	2.95

   If you order 5 cases from the above supplier and take advantage of his discount terms, what will be the value of the invoice raised?

3. After taking stock you find the value to be £1765. During the period the food purchases were £6879 and the value of the food stocks at the beginning of the period were £2740. Food supplied to the bars amounted to £27 and food used to feed the staff was £458. Sales for the period were £14156. (Ignore VAT.)

   (a) What was the value of the cost of food used?

   (b) What was the value of the cost of food sold?

   (c) What was the gross profit for the period?

   (d) What was the kitchen percentage for the period?

   (e) What was the shortfall/surplus for the period in money terms if the budgeted gross profit percentage was 60%?

7
Beverage Control and Costing

Introduction

In a small unit selling beverages, three main problems present themselves: (i) ensuring that every invoice is noted; (ii) keeping separate records for separate bars; (iii) avoiding fraud.

We shall deal with each of these in turn.

Ensuring that every invoice is noted

It is essential that every invoice detailing supplies to the establishment has been noted and taken account of, because the *exact* purchases for any given trading period are needed for the stocktaker to prepare his figures. Any omission will have the effect of decreasing the purchase figure and thus, on paper, will increase the gross profit. Management may then continue in a euphoric state, unaware of the establishment's shortcomings! Office routine should be strict, with delivery notes checked against invoices, invoices checked against statements, and each stocktaking period's documentation kept together.

Consider the following example. In Example (1) all the invoices have been accounted for but in Example (2) one invoice to the value of £500 has been 'lost'.

Example 1			*Example 2*	
Opening stock	£5000		Opening stock	£5000
+ Purchases	3500		+ Purchases (one	3000
(Invoices)	———		omission of £500)	———
	8500			8000
− Closing stock	4700		− Closing stock	4700
= Cost of sales	3800		= Cost of sales	3300

If the total sales for the period were £6500 then in Example (1) the gross profit would be £2700 and in Example (2) £3200. It is perhaps worth mentioning that when a stocktaking result shows an unexpectedly high profit, investigation should take place to try and find out the reason. There is even a possibility that should the invoice never come to light the business will pay income tax to the Inland Revenue on profit it has never earned.

The stocktaker may spot errors in invoicing by noticing increases in particular products for which there is no invoice. For example: if the opening stock of Scotch whisky was 10 bottles and the closing stock was 30 bottles, one would expect that amongst the invoices would be one showing a delivery of Scotch whisky. If there was not, then the indication is that an invoice is missing.

Assuming that all the documentation is correct and complete, the stocktaker can extract the exact purchase figure for the period and, in addition, make alterations to the record of cost prices, thus producing accurate valuations and suggest retail price alterations where necessary.

Keeping separate records for separate bars

Bar and cellar stocks are usually treated as one. Shortages, therefore, cannot be isolated to any one department, but are only regarded as a general symptom of fraud.

Once a large shortage does occur, management are prompted to institute detailed requisitioning procedures. It is interesting to note that the same does not usually occur when a large surplus has been made! However, even then, problems arise because of borrowing from one bar to another in cases of emergency without noting the transaction, lending stock to outside catering establishments, working a bar with many varied staff during days off and meal times, and even lending barmen the cellar keys to obtain supplies when management are taken up with other 'important' matters.

It is possible to isolate deficiencies within the establishment, but considerable effort is required and the question of value should be looked at. If the deficiency is £10 over a period of one month, is it worth spending £50 worth of time finding where the error was? At first glance the answer may well be no, but perhaps £50 spent now will save £10 a month for the next five years.

Some establishments institute a 'control by elimination' procedure, where management may first control the cellar by splitting it into its component sections: draught beers, bottled beers, wines, spirits, minerals and tobacco. Deliveries are checked by management (very often theft has taken place before the stock arrives at the establishment) and containers which often represent more in value than the products they contain are kept locked, with care taken to ensure that the correct credit is given on their return to the supplier. Supplies from the cellar can then be controlled separately to individual bars, even to the extent of preparing individual stocktaking results for each bar. The stocktaking periods can be reduced from (say) one month to one week. In more extreme cases this period can be further reduced to one day or part of day, and on occasions it has been known to reduce the stocktaking period down to a meal break so that an individual member of staff can be isolated.

Avoiding fraud

Management should be aware of the areas where fraud is possible and take every precaution to ensure that any loop-hole is closed. We now deal with the principal methods of fraud which management should be particularly concerned with.

Dilution. Dilution is the addition of water (usually) to spirits — particularly gin, vodka and white rum. It has even been known for a barman simply to wipe the rim of the glass with gin and serve a measure of water! It is illegal to dilute alcoholic beverages and management should be aware of the fact that they are also held responsible if a member of their staff is guilty of this offence. Stocktakers should make periodic checks on the specific gravity of spirits using a hydrometer. HM Customs and Excise and Weights and Measures Inspectors will also make their own checks. Members of the public are also at liberty to remove samples for testing by the public analyst.

Adulteration. Adulteration is the substitution of one product for another. For example cheap draught sherry may be put into an expensive bottle and sold at a higher price as a brand leader. Management and customers should check the colour of the product, and its smell and taste. Concern should also be shown when a member of staff is seen filling empty bottles.

Carrying In. Staff supplying their own spirits and removing the cost and profit from takings are guilty of 'carrying in'. Fraud of this nature would not be detected by stocktaking and is, of course, not only defrauding the business but also the Inland Revenue and the Customs and Excise. Strict cash control should be in evidence together with some control of staff bags, etc. It is also possible to control the empty and full bottles kept on the premises, and some establishments even stamp all spirit bottles on receipt from suppliers with the establishment stamp, so that 'strangers' are immediately noticed. Back-up stocks should also be controlled – one 'on optic' and one spare is a reasonable system.

'Reduced-profit' Drinks. This method of fraud involves recording a bottle of spirit as being sold 'off sale' when, in fact, it was sold through an optic. Using a 6-out optic a standard bottle of spirit will yield 31.5 measures. If the bar price per measure is 65p, then one bottle will produce £20.47 in takings. If that bottle is recorded as being sold for £7.50 'off sale' then it can be seen that £12.97 can be 'creamed off'. The areas to look at and control are fluctuations in sales and the relationship between spirit sales and mixers. Evidence of empty quarter- or half-bottles in the bottle bin should also be investigated since these would only be sold 'off sale'.

Mixed Drinks. Fraud can occur where incorrect quantities are given to a customer who has ordered a mixed drink or cocktail. If it is done accidentally, then the result will be a beverage surplus. Standard recipes play their part here as in the kitchen, together with the provision of the correct equipment and staff training. Take note of any complaints by customers.

Short Measuring. This needs little in the way of explanation. The correct equipment should be provided and the staff made aware of the legal implications of short-measuring and the fact that customer goodwill can be lost.

Short Changing. This is often accidental, particularly with large denomination notes. Strict control of cash is necessary.

Overcharging. This, like short changing, is often accidental. Staff fond of this particular type of fraud usually reserve the overcharging to the large 'rounds' of drinks. Pay attention to your customers. Staff training plays its part as does strict control of cash with particular reference to till checks and till rolls.

Use of Friends. Staff often like to give away drinks to friends — sometimes as a gift for helping the staff carry in liquor. Because of this, some establishments restrict staff and their friends from using the facilities of the establishment.

Stock Inflation. Shortage of stock may be covered up by the *temporary* introduction of extra stock or even the substitution of stock, such as cold tea for Scotch. The fraud usually comes to light over a period of time as the deficiency builds up.

Cigarettes. The removal of stock from a kitchen may well be considered to be 'fair game' — a sandwich eaten in the still room does not usually warrant dismissal; a barman who takes a packet of cigarettes is guilty of fraud. The advantages of removing items like cigarettes are many, but principally the item is small, light, acceptable and expensive. Why do so many public houses now have cigarette machines?

In addition to the problems mentioned above, some of which may well come to light after a stocktaking exercise, there are other problems the caterer faces when dealing with beverages.

Ullage, or beverages which for one reason or another cannot be sold, is one issue. An establishment selling traditional ale will experience greater problems with beer ullage than an establishment selling only keg beer. (Was that one reason for the move to keg beers in the 1960s?) Some allowance must be made for ullage by management: there are bound to be accidents (should a record be kept?), and the pipes must be cleaned at least once a week which means that the beer in the pipe is wasted. Particular care should be taken to see that waste does not creep to an unacceptable level – gas pressures should be maintained at correct levels, temperature control should be efficient, equipment should be clean (particularly glasses), and staff should be trained. Particular attention should be paid to the serving of strong-tasting drinks such as Pernod. If a measure which has been used for Pernod is then used for gin, without thorough washing, the drink will be unacceptable. Physical checks should be made on leaking optics and some investigation made into the cause of errors.

Control tends to fall back on the overall result of stocktaking. This will, at least, force management to worry about making sure all cash is returned and all allowances noted.

A psychological play on control procedure will, in itself, create staff respect with regard to mangement's efforts towards efficiency.

We now turn to the method of control.

Control of beverages

Any form of control should have the following features:
(i)   retail prices should be controlled;
(ii) sales should be reduced, whenever possible, to a cash basis and credit sales carefully checked to accounts or bills;
(iii) the cellar should be kept under the direct administration of management, with manual help.

We now examine these features in turn.

Retail price control

The following table shows how many portion sizes should be yielded by a bottle.

Portion size	Product	Yield
6-out measure	75 cl spirit or aperitif	31.5
3-out measure	75 cl spirit or aperitif	15.75
6-out measure	1.13 ltr spirit	47
4 fl oz	75 cl wine	6.5
5 fl oz	75 cl wine	5.2
4 fl oz	1 litre wine, etc.	8.75
5 fl oz	1 litre wine, etc.	7

Once the portion size has been set, the selling price can be determined in much the same way as for food prices, i.e.

$$\frac{\text{Beverage cost per portion}}{\text{Beverage cost percentage}} \times 100 = \text{Selling price}$$

Examples

(1)   A bottle of Scotch costs £5.50, exclusive of VAT. The gross profit percentage required is 60% and VAT is to be charged at 15%. If the portion size is to be 1 × 6-out measure, what will the retail price be?

$$\text{Cost per portion} = \frac{7.50}{31} = 24.19 \text{ p}$$

$$\text{Selling price} = \frac{24.19}{40} \times 100$$

$$= 60.475 \text{ p}$$

$$\text{Now add VAT at 15\%: VAT} = \frac{60.475}{100} \times 15$$

$$= \frac{907.125}{100}$$

$$= 9.07$$

Therefore, the selling price will be:

$$60.475 + 9.07$$

$$= 69.545 \ (70 \ p)$$

(N.B. When considering 'rounding' up or down of figures it is accepted by most people that you 'round' up when the figure is 0.5 or above and 'round' down when it is 0.4 or below. When preparing selling prices, particularly when using a calculator, it is best to 'round' up or down just once, at the end of the calculation, and not during the calculation stages.)

(2)   Wine by the glass is to be sold in 5 fl oz quantities, and costs £2.00 per litre, exclusive of VAT. What will be the retail price per glass if the gross profit percentage required is 70% and VAT is to be charged at 15%? (N.B. Refer to the table on page 101.)

$$\text{Portion cost} = \frac{2.00}{7} = 28.57 \ p$$

$$\text{Selling price} = \frac{28.57}{30} \times 100 + 15\%$$

$$= \frac{2857}{30} + 15\%$$

$$= 95.23 + 15\%$$

$$= 95.23 + 14.28$$

$$= 109.5 \ p$$

$$\text{or } 110 \ p \text{ (rounded)}$$

Stocktaking

All stocks of unused or part used stock are valued at cost price (exclusive of VAT). Particular attention should be paid to the valuation of containers, since these now represent a large cash value, often larger than the value of their contents.

The physical layout of the cellar should relate to the entries made in the stocktaker's books.

The *estimation* of the stock remaining in the bars may be calculated in different ways, according to the preference of the stocktaker. He may use a graduated ruler for the various shapes and sizes of bottles or by guessing the volumes remaining.

When guessing the contents, inaccuracies may occur. So long as the stocktaker allows for compensating error, off-setting overestimation against underestimation, the result will be almost as accurate as that produced by the most careful measurement.

Estimation of part full bottles may be done by:

(i)   Estimation of the number of 'tots' remaining.

(ii)   Estimation of the fraction remaining. The most used fractions being 1/8ths and 1/10ths. There is a greater possibility of error when using either very small fractions (e.g. 1/16ths) or very large fractions (e.g. halves).

Results are usually written down by indicating full bottles with large numbers and part-full bottles by indicating a small number with a small line underneath. Successive part-full bottles are added together. A decimal point indicates the end of the count in part of the bar.

Example

Using fractions of 1/8th, the count in the picture above would be as follows:

$2\underline{3} . 1 . 1 . 3\underline{6} . = 8$ bottles and 1/8th bottle

The value is then determined by multiplying the number of bottles, after first converting the fraction to a decimal, by the cost price exclusive of VAT. (The VAT is not taken into account since it is claimed back from HM Customs and Excise — see Chapter 10.)

An example of a stocktaker's sheet may be:

Cost £ p	Product	Stock remaining	Total	Valuation £ p
5.20	Prop. Scotch	$1^6.3.12.3^2.1^3$	21^3	111 15

The total value of stock is then calculated by addition, and the value of consumption calculated as follows:

Opening stock + Purchases − Closing stock = Cost of consumption

Example
What is the value of the closing stock, given the following information?

Cost £ p	Product	Stock Remaining	Total	Valuation £ p
5.15	Prop. Scotch	$3^3.16.1^4.$	20^7	107 51
3.20	Manzanilla	$20.3^7.$	23^7	76 40
2.94	Amontillado	$6.2.1^1.2^4.$	11^5	34 18
3.68	Oloroso	$5.1^1.$	6^1	22 54
8.25	V.S.O.P.	$2.1^6.$	3^6	30 94
7.56	Cognac ***	$1.1^5.$	2^5	19 85
2.10	Pale ale	$6.3^7.2^4.$	11^{11}	25 03
18.20	Real ale	$18.4.7.$	29	58 64
				375 09

Notes
(i)   The fraction used in taking stock was ⅛ths.

(ii) Bottled beers are counted in dozens; therefore 4^7 = 55 bottles. (Note though that some breweries are now supplying pint bottles in cases of 15. Where this happens it is perhaps better to count individual bottles and record one single figure.)

(iii)   Keg beer in this example has been counted in gallons and the cost price given is per firkin (9 gallons).

Stocktaking results will show the value, at cost, of the stock used (sold?) during the accounting period. This figure is then subtracted from the takings figure to reveal the gross profit, which is then compared with the sales to produce the gross profit percentage.

On occasions, this percentage will either fall below the target percentage (deficiency) or exceed the target (surplus). Depending upon the size of the discrepancy, attention should be paid to the following factors, any one of which may account for the variation.

Ullage. This is due to draught beers, fobbing, pipe cleaning, broken bottles, returned drinks, faulty optics, incorrectly mixed drinks, poor cleaning techniques, incorrect cellar temperature, incorrect temperature setting on flash coolers.

Sales Mix. This may be due to spirits being sold 'off sale' and tobacco sales — both of which produce very low gross profit percentages.

Approved Entertaining. Perhaps management had a party — were all the drinks recorded? Should there be an entertainment book?

Breakages. Perhaps the unopened necks of broken bottles should be kept?

Inter-bar Transfers. If the recording of an inter-bar transfer has not taken place then, usually, one bar will be showing a surplus and another a compensating deficiency. This is, of course, not the case if stock has been lent outside the establishment.

Accounting. Sales may have been omitted or invoices not received or lost. The method of valuation of stock should also be taken into consideration and stock should be valued at its historic cost (but this is not always possible). If stock has been revalued (perhaps because of a budget increase) then on paper the establishment will have made a surplus profit. This of course, may well be intentional.

Containers. Deposits may have been incorrectly charged or removed from the premises without a note of credit. This is now 'big money' and considerable care should be taken to ensure that all containers are correctly charged for and credited. (We know of one public house which stored its empties in the car park and noticed one young man collect a selection and return them to the counter for the 'money back'. The licensee then put them back in the car park where the young man collected them again and returned them to the counter!)

Credit Notes not Received. Credit notes may not have been received for products returned to suppliers or products short on delivery.

EXERCISE 44

1. Sherry is to be sold in 3-out portion sizes. The cost price is £2.55 per standard bottle exclusive of VAT. What will the selling price be if the gross profit percentage is to be 50% and VAT is charged at 15%?

2. A firkin (9 gallon) keg of beer costs £17.40 exclusive of VAT. What will the selling price per pint be if the gross profit percentage is to be 33% and VAT is charged at 15%?

3. A member of staff, unknown to management, is consistently but not deliberately, giving incorrect change to customers. Explain the possible ways this problem might come to light and the effects on the stocktaking result.

4. Draught sherry, costing £32.50 per 5 gallons, exclusive of VAT is to be sold in 3-out and 1½ out measures (glass and schooner). What will the retail price be if the gross profit percentage is to be 45% and VAT is to be charged at 15%?

5. Bottled lager costs £2.75 per dozen, exclusive of VAT. What will the retail price per bottle be after allowing 15% VAT and so that a gross profit of 40% is made?

6. The value of stock on 1 May was £546.20 and the purchases for the period 1 May to 31 May were £1276.40. During the same period the bar takings were £2376.30. (All these figures are exclusive of VAT.)

   Value the following closing stock, taken on 31 May and determine:

   (a) The cost of consumption.
   (b) The actual gross profit made.
   (c) The gross profit percentage.
   (d) If the target gross profit percentage was 45% what was the surplus or deficiency?

Cost £ p	Product	Stock remaining	Total	Valuation £ p
2.20	Martini	$2^4.3^1.6.$		
3.40	Cinzano	$1^2.5^3.4.$		
4.75	Scotch	$12.3^1.2^5.1^1.$		
6.56	Cognac	$8.^14.2.1.^4.$		
8.86	V.S.O.P.	$5.2.^7.$		
17.20	Keg beer	$40.6.7.$		
3.20	Pale ale	$4^3.6^4.14^8.$		

Note that bottled beers are counted in dozens and keg beer is costed per 10 gallons. All other spirits and aperitifs are estimated in 1/8ths.

8
Department Control of Non-perishable Items

Introduction

Whilst most establishments keep tight control on food and beverage operations, other forms of departmental control are non-existent, or half-heartedly imposed because staff feel that the effort involved isn't worth the saving as it doesn't affect them. With the terrific increase in the cost of

cleaning agents,
replacement of equipment (silver, glasses, vacuum cleaners),
refurbishing (furniture, decoration, soft furnishing),
repairs and servicing,
energy,

profit margins can soon be eroded away and a greater return can be achieved on capital by investing it than running a catering establishment. Therefore, more attention should be paid to analysing the costs involved and seeing if they can be reduced by any form of control. A lot of the same rules apply but the application is a little different.

Cleaning agents

No matter how well planned and equipped the establishment is and how well trained the staff are, if the principles of good purchasing when requisitioning and ordering of cleaning agents are not observed, all will be lost. Firstly there is a need to analyse each type of cleaning agent used:

(i)   What is it used for?

(ii)   What is it supposed to do?

(iii) Can the same result be achieved any other way?

(iv)   If so, are the alternatives (a) more labour-intensive? (b) more difficult? (c) why aren't they being used?

(v)   Are there any other products on the market and ways of cleaning that do the same job? Is the result (a) as good?, (b) better but more expensive and time-consuming?

(vi)   What does it cost in terms of labour and cleaning agents to keep an area clean?

(vii) Is all the cleaning that is being done necessary and at the present frequency?

(viii) Is the best, in fact, too good?

A cleaning agent should improve the operation and reduce the cost whilst maintaining and protecting the surface without increasing the effort or labour involvement. This type of analysis can only be achieved by running controlled tests and studying the results. Often a lot of cleaning operations are carried out as a matter of habit and routine rather than as a result of work scheduling; by contrast some cleaning is neglected to such an extent that when it has to be done it is very expensive and labour-intensive, a little and often is a good guide-line.

When a cleaning agent has been selected it is important to know how long a stated amount will last while constantly achieving the required finish. This is a very difficult thing to establish and has to be worked out as an average. While the policy of only giving a full container in return for an empty one does seem to offer some form of control, the frequency of change needs to be controlled. But it must be related to use. Otherwise staff will get uptight if they have done extra work for you and are then refused a replacement!

For dish washing and laundry washing the amount of cleaning agent added can be controlled electronically and the type used can be analysed to relate to the water and temperature being used and the soiling to be removed. Though it may be expensive to install initially, the cost saving can pay for itself many times over. Consideration should also be given to whether a water softener will reduce wear and tear on the machinery, items being cleansed and usage of cleaning agent.

Exactly the same forms for control of cleaning agent stock can be utilised, and some establishments hold cleaning agents in their main stores and the different departments requisition them as they are required. Each department then controls its own issuing and usage.

Some further words of warning are in order here about the purchasing of cleaning agents especially where this is done by contract or as a result of a committee, without specialist cleaning knowledge, who may be tempted to use products as a result of tenders or because they are cheaper.

(i)   The dilution rates of the commodities need to be compared.

(ii)   Their efficiency needs to be established.

(iii)   Some cleaning agents and care products are not compatible when used in conjunction with each other. This can result in a poor finish or even damage to a surface.

In fact, the purchasing of cleaning agents requires a specialist knowledge and should not be undertaken without trained advice, as unnecessary expense and untold damage can result.

Replacement of equipment

If equipment is not hired, more has to be purchased as a result of loss, misuse, damage or from wear and tear. It is sensible and prudent to analyse both the need for replacement, why and how often it needs replacing, and also to think about the need for that particular item. For example, if a restaurant is desperately short of sweet plates but has a stock of fish plates, it might be a sensible time to rethink the place settings and crockery usage and introduce a more standardised approach to the range. This also applies to glasses for use behind the bar and in the food service area. Cutlery is another 'disaster area' as far as replacement frequency is concerned, particularly teaspoons. Two questions can be asked about this — firstly, should the same expensive product be used for this item, and secondly, could loss be reduced by allocating each area a stated stock which it is accountable for daily or weekly? The rate of replacement of table linen, if not hired, also gives cause for concern mainly because of misuse. How many times a day can napkins be observed being used as ovencloths, shoe-shiners, tea towels and chefs' kerchiefs? Again, thought should be given to the use of disposable paper items and a costing exercise carried out or a trial month of trading be operated so that customer reaction and operating costs can be established. An aspect not often related to the misuse of table linen is the provision of the correct cloths and in the necessary amounts. This is now aggravated by the linen room no longer having available worn items which can be recycled as cleaning cloths. These cloths were often more efficient than the purchased items. Because linen is hired it doesn't mean to say that responsibility for its use can be ignored as some hire companies do include a surcharge for loss and damaged items.

Refurbishing

A well-organised establishment will have a programme of renovation and redecoration. When new surfaces and furnishings are being selected it is important that consideration should be given to the design of the item, the finish it has, the ease of cleaning, and whether it is hard-wearing and serviceable. If a complete renovation is planned for rescheming, a mock-up of the new room plan is a sensible idea so that problems can be spotted before the goods are ordered and installed. Some thought also needs to be given to work simplification: can fitments be cantilevered to ease cleaning; are all the crevices and flat surfaces in the room necessary, or can they be planned out? This may involve capital expenditure at the time but could be cost-effective in labour terms. Can the new surfaces be selected so that they do not require expensive cleaning agents or time-consuming cleaning operations to maintain them or a longer period between renovation?

Repairs and servicing

The Health and Safety at Work Act now legislates that accurate records should be kept concerning maintenance and servicing of mechanical and electrical equipment. The training of staff in the use of this equipment is also controlled. Maintenance costs can be considerably reduced if routine checks and simple servicing, such as oiling, blade-sharpening, temperature adjustments, are carried out regularly. Inefficient equipment can be time-consuming: a vacuum cleaner will not pick up bits if the bag is full; the right number of slices will not be obtained from a leg of lamb if the slice adjuster does not work or the blade is not sharp so it 'rags' the meat; the whole content of an old-style deep freeze can be lost if it is not regularly defrosted, or the bulb indicating malfunction is not checked to see that it is operational; dirty burners in a central heating system will increase fuel consumption. It is obviously in the management's interest to control the overhead costs because every penny saved here is immediately reflected in the net profit figure.

Saving energy

We all know these days that energy is scarce and expensive, and that we should all try to 'save it'. There are many ways in which energy consumption can be reduced and controlled, some of which receive financial help from the Government, though staff training and incentive schemes can also help.

The kitchen often wastes energy. How often are ovens lit first thing in the morning to warm the kitchen and left on till closedown though not being used! Grills are often lit and left on for hours. In fact, somebody who suggested that time controls should be fitted to certain items of kitchen equipment was given a £2000 payment because the implementation of the idea in RAF camps throughout the country had saved over £200 000 p.a. in fuel consumption. A hotel group also reduced its electricity bill just by fitting bulbs over the door to the rooms on one side of the corridor instead of both sides, which gave an adequate light at half the cost. Thermostats on boilers and in rooms can also reduce energy consumption. If planning new extensions, make sure each floor is zoned so that it can be isolated without any problem and make sure reception lets rooms in heated zones only during slack periods or redecoration.

In order that the staff become as control-conscious as the management, some forms of incentive should be offered. Larger organisations run interdepartmental competitions and the winning department is given a wage bonus equal to a percentage of the saving, or some other award. Certainly the attitude should be encouraged that there are benefits from saving and not as in some organisations that any monies saved should be expended no matter what, as next year's budget figures will be reduced by the amount the economies have achieved and the departmental head be given a wrap over the knuckles!

Fuel bills

Checking of fuel consumption fuel bills should be done regularly and some saving may be effected if the tariffs offered by the various boards are analysed to see if the establishment could be advantageously transferred. Also it might be possible to route some of the electricity through the off-peak meter for corridor and other areas needing to be lit all through the night.

Fuel consumption is charged according to the number of units used at a price according to the tariff of the establishment. This tariff can be made up of either a standing charge plus the value of units consumed or a sliding scale with a high price for the first units consumed and a lower rate for the remainder, or other terms are available on Commercial Tariffs on application to the relative board.

Examples
(1) Tariff 1. Find the cost of using 13 780 therms of gas on the Domestic Tariff. Standing charge per quarter: £6.35. Cost per therm 36.30 p.

	£ p
Standing charge per quarter	6.35
13 780 therms at 36.30	5002.14
	£5008.49

(2) Find the cost of using 21 792 units of electricity (15 792 units used between 7 pm and 7 am on Tariff 7). Standing charge: £6.35. Units used between 7 pm and 7 am, 2.25 p, all other units 5.52 p.

		£ p
Standing charge per quarter	=	6.35
15 792 units at 2.25 p	=	355.32
(21 792 − 15 792) units at 5.52 p	=	331.20
		£692.87

EXERCISE 45

A business produced the following figures for a month's trading.

	£
Food purchases	6030
Laundry	62
Fuel	329
Cleaning agents	129
Maintenance and servicing	58
Replacement of glass	450

Sales for the month were £11800. By control methods the following percentage savings were achieved:

1% on food purchase

$\frac{1}{2}$% on laundry

$2\frac{1}{2}$% on fuel

$\frac{1}{4}$% on cleaning agents

Nothing on maintenance and servicing
1% on replacement of glass.

1. What was the effect on the month's profit?

2. What percentage of sales is this?

3. What was the gross profit percentage with control?

9
Wages and Income Tax

Introduction

The majority of catering employees are paid on a fixed basis for the work they have done. They may be paid weekly, or monthly if they are employed on a full-time basis, or daily if they are part-time. Generally speaking, employees paid on a weekly or daily basis are said to receive a *wage* and those on a monthly basis receive a *salary*.

Hotels and catering establishments, including public houses, restaurants, clubs and industrial establishments are obliged to pay their work force certain minimum rates of pay for the job. Since there is very little trade union activity within catering, the problem of deciding what these basic minimum rates should be rests with the Government and is enforced by updating, from time to time, the Wages Order. This Order sets out the basic hourly rate to be paid to catering workers who are over the age of 21. Staff under 21 are now placed in the position of negotiating their rates with their individual employer.

A copy of this Order, and information supplied by the Catering Wages Councils must be available to all members of staff within an establishment, and it is usually to be found hanging on or near the staff notice board. It is probably fair to say that market forces generally prevail and, in areas of high unemployment, employers will be paying rates nearer to the prescribed basic, with this rate being increased in areas where recruitment is more difficult.

A great number of workers within catering are paid a fixed sum of money for a pre-determined number of hours work per week. It is then often agreed that work in excess of the basic week will be paid on an hourly basis at higher rates. For example: a chef may be paid £100 per week for a 40-hour week. For the first 4 hours over the 40, he could receive time and a quarter; for the next 4, time and a half; and any hours over 48, double time.

It then becomes a mathematical problem, at the end of the week, to calculate the chef's basic entitlement. If, for example, one week he worked 50 hours then his gross wage would be made up as follows:

	£ p
Basic Pay (40 hours)	100.00
4 hours at $1\frac{1}{4}$ (3.12)	12.50
4 hours at $1\frac{1}{2}$ (3.75)	15.00
2 hours at double (5.00).	10.00
Gross pay	£137.50

Unfortunately the chef will not actually take this sum of money home with him. He will be required to contribute some of it to the Government, in the form of Income Tax, and some of it to the Department of Health and Social Security, so that when he retires he will receive a pension, or when he is ill receive medical help, or if he is out of work receive financial help until such time as he can find another job.

115

PAYE (Pay As You Earn)

The PAYE system was introduced so that deductions of income tax from an employee could keep pace with his earnings. In other words he could pay a little each week or month instead of facing a very large bill at the end of the year. The system does work both ways in as much as the Government receive their tax at regular intervals and since most people tend to spend all their earnings (if not more) the Inland Revenue are aware that should they leave the collecting of income tax to the end of the year they may well find considerable difficulty in getting it!

It works like this. Everybody is allowed to earn a certain amount of money free of tax, this is called a *personal allowance,* and it tends to vary from year to year according to the whim of the Chancellor. In the year 1988/89 for example, the personal allowance for a single person was fixed at £2605 per year, or £50.10 per week. For the same year, a married man was allowed £4095 per year or £78.75 per week. In addition to this personal allowance the Inland Revenue allow certain of your expenses to be earned free of tax. The sort of thing that is currently allowed is interest paid on a mortgage to buy a house, interest paid on a loan to improve certain features of a house, a subscription to a professional body concerned with your work, the purchase of a uniform or overall for work, and so on.

Each year the Inland Revenue add up all these personal allowances and from the resulting figure, issue a Code Number. If, for example, a person's allowances came to £2453 for the year, then the Inland Revenue would issue a Code Number: 245. After the number they very often put a letter, the most common being L, H, or T. These letters simply indicate how the allowances were calculated and will allow a code to be changed quickly should there be a change in the amount of the allowance. The letter L, for example, indicates that the person was given the lower allowance (single persons), the letter H indicates the higher allowance (married man), and the letter T is issued where there are special circumstances. Some people, who do not wish their employer to receive their code with a letter L or H on it, can ask the Inland Revenue to substitute the letter T.

Having decided the personal allowance (or tax free pay), the Inland Revenue divide this figure by 52 if wages are earned weekly or by 12 in the case of monthly-paid workers. Thus, a person's weekly or monthly tax-free pay is calculated. At each pay period this amount of tax-free pay is deducted from the employee's gross pay and given to him intact. Of the remainder, if there is any, a proportion is removed in the form of tax and the remainder given to the employee. The amount of tax paid on this remaining portion is calculated on an annual basis.

Example

A man earns £125 per week and is allowed £1465 per year by the Inland Revenue as his personal allowance.

His personal allowance computes down to £28.17 per week and, therefore, he would be taxed as follows:

	£ p
Basic gross pay	125.00
Less allowance	28.17
Taxable pay	£ 96.83
Basic rate tax deducted at 25%	£24.21

The man's take home pay would therefore be:

	£ p
	125.00
Less income tax	24.21
	£100.79

In 1988 the basic rate of tax was 25% and from time to time the Government alter the basic rates of tax and/or the amount of personal allowances given to individuals. It can be seen, from the above example that the higher a person's personal allowance, the less tax he will pay; and it is worth pointing out that when a man gets married he is allowed a higher personal allowance (one of the few financial advantages to marriage but at the moment only applicable to men)

National Insurance

In addition to income tax, National Insurance contributions must be paid by most employees. Those who earn low incomes (less than approximately £39 per week) are exempt, but everybody else must pay according to their income, rather like income tax. As has already been mentioned, this payment is for things like the employee's pension, and not only does the employee pay but his employer also contributes on his behalf. National Insurance (Graduated National Insurance, GNIC) is also deducted on each pay date and sent, on the employee's behalf, to the Inland Revenue.

Tax deduction cards

At each pay day the employer will record all the details of an employee's earnings, Tax-free pay, National Insurance Contributions and Income Tax paid on a Tax Deduction Card. Tax Deduction Cards are also issued, free of charge, by the Inland Revenue if the employer prefers, and are given the form number P11.

A typical Tax Deduction Card is reproduced below:

						TAX DEDUCTION CARD													
1			**2**		**3**			**4**		**5**		**6**		**7**		**8**		**9**	
National Insurance Contributions						Month No.	Week No.	Pay in week or month		Total pay to date		Total free pay to date		Total taxable pay to date		Total tax due to date		Tax deducted or refunded in week	
Total Employee + employer payable		Employee contbtns payable		Employee contbtns contract out															
£	p	£	p	£	p			£	p	£	p	£	p	£	p	£	p	£	p
						1	1												
							2												
							3												
						2	4												
							5												
							6												
							7												
						3	8												
							9												
							10												
							11												
						4	12												
							13												
							14												
							15												
						5	16												
							17												
							18												
							19												
						6	20												
							21												
							22												

Each employee has a Tax Deduction Card and there are usually spaces available for all the personal details about the employee. You fill in a card as follows.

(i)   Enter in column 4 the gross pay for the week or month.

(ii)   Add the figure just entered in column 4 to the last figure appearing in column 5 (so that in week 2 the figure appearing in column 5 will be this week's day plus last week's pay; and so on).

(iii)   Enter in column 6 the tax-free pay allowed so far this year. This can be found by referring to the Inland Revenue Free Pay Tables under the appropriate week number, and looking up the appropriate code number for the employee.

(iv)   Deduct the figure you have just entered in column 6 from the total in column 5 and record the answer in column 7.

(v)   Look up the figure you have just entered in column 7 in the Inland Revenue Taxable Pay Tables and read off the amount of tax due to date. Enter this amount in column 8.

(vi)   The figure appearing immediately above the one you have just written in column 8 is the amount of tax which the employee has already paid. The figure you have just written is the tax due to date. Subtract the figure above from the figure below and enter the result in column 9 — this is the amount of tax the employee will have to pay this week. However, if the figure above, in column 8, is larger than the one you have just written, then subtract normally and record the answer in column 9, but this time it will be a refund of tax. This figure would normally either be recorded in brackets or marked with an 'R' to indicate that it is being returned to the employee and not deducted.

(vii)   The entries appearing in columns 1, 2 and 3 are found by referring to Graduated National Insurance Tables and reading off the deductions against the gross wage of the employee for this period.

Government tax forms

There are many Government tax forms, but listed below are the ones the reader is most likely to come into contact with. Anybody employing staff will be issued with the tax forms they require, free of charge, with additional forms should they run short or expand their operation.

P11. Tax Deduction Card (similar to the one illustrated).

P45. Notification to the Inland Revenue that an employee has left. This form is in three parts, part one being sent to the local Inland Revenue office as soon as an employee leaves. The employee takes part two and three to his next employer, who, having completed an additional section, retains part two in his records and sends part three to his local Inland Revenue office.

P46. Notification to the Inland Revenue of an employee starting work who does not have parts two and three of a form P45.

P1. The Tax Return Form sent to all employees. The employee has an obligation to complete this form, giving details of all his income and expenses, and return it to the Inland Revenue within 30 days. Failure to complete the form may well result in the employee paying too much income tax since the Inland Revenue will not be aware of his status.

P60. A Statement of Pay and Tax Deducted for the past year. Every employee will receive a P60 usually within one month from April 5th. The employee should check the information on this form and in cases of error the employee should take the matter up with his employer. Should the employee wish to check with the tax tables, then these are available at the public library or the local tax office are able to make their own review of the case.

Tax and the self- employed

The profits from a business within catering, such as a public house, restaurant or hotel, are normally assessed under Schedule D Case 1. Caterers, operating normally should produce annual accounts prepared by an accountant. These will normally be in three parts: (i) The Trading Account (so that the business can determine its gross profit percentages and/or kitchen percentage), (ii) the Profit and Loss Account, and (iii) a Balance Sheet.

The profit (net) shown by the business account will usually form the basis of a tax assessment, but the Inland Revenue may well make one or two adjustments. In simple terms the Inland Revenue will allow the proprietor to deduct from his gross profit the expenses of the business. By reducing the profit the proprietor will pay less tax, and, therefore the Inland Revenue are careful as to what they allow to be removed. In general terms they will not allow any of the following:

(i)   any payment or expense not wholly paid out for the purposes of the business,

(ii)   any payment or expense paid out for the private purpose of the proprietor,

(iii) any loss not connected with the business,

(iv)   entertaining expenses unless connected with foreign customers,

(v)   fines for illegal acts, or any legal expense connected with them,

(vi)   any donations to charity or political parties.

In addition to the points mentioned above, the Inland Revenue will also expect the resident proprietor of a catering business to contribute towards his own home. When the profits have been agreed by the Inland Revenue they will add on to them a proportion of the fuel costs for private use, a proportion of the rent (if any), rates and loan interest. If the business is a public house or restaurant, they will also be interested to know if you have charged the food consumed by the proprietor or his family to the business, and whether or not the proprietor and his family paid for their beverages, cigarettes, etc.

All this tax assessment must, of course, take place after the event. In other words, the Inland Revenue cannot demand payment of tax on profits until those profits have been earned. The effect is that the self-employed businessman will pay his income tax on profits during the year following the earning of those profits.

EXERCISE 46

1. A waiter is employed on a 40-hour week basis for which the agreed wage is £60. It is also agreed that for the first four hours of overtime he will be paid at the rate of time and a quarter; the next four hours at time and threequarters, and all subsequent hours at double time. What will be his gross pay if in one week he works 58 hours?

2. A man has a personal tax allowance of £985 and in addition is allowed £28 being a fee to a professional body, £645 mortgage interest and £54 loan interest to extend his house. What will his Tax Code Number be and how much per week can he earn before he starts paying income tax?

3. If the current tax rates are 25% on the first £750 taxable income and 30% on the next £7250, how much will a person with a taxable income of £3200 in a year have to pay in income tax?

4. A man has a Code Number of 245H and is paid £7500 per annum. Assuming the same tax rates as for Question 3, how much will the man pay in income tax over the course of the year?

10
Value Added Tax

Introduction

Value Added Tax (or VAT) was introduced into the United Kingdom on April Fool's Day 1973! It replaced Purchase Tax which, in the past, had been added to selling prices by retailers. The reason for the introduction of the tax was to bring this country into line with other Common Market countries.

When it was first introduced the Government fixed the rate at 10% and since then the rate has gone up and down. In 1980, it was changed to 15%.

All caterers must register as a VAT trader if their sales exceed £21 300 per annum. Below this figure the caterer has the option to register or not. The ramifications on the catering industry were, and are, great; not the least because the tax has the effect of increasing nearly all catering prices by the rate of the tax (before, this was not the case).

Put into very simple terms, any goods or services provided by a caterer to a customer are subjected to the tax, the only exception being where the caterer has sold something without adding his profit to it which was not subject to the tax in the first place, such as a newspaper, recorded as a VPO (Various Paid Out) by receptionists.

The administration of the tax is taken care of by the Department of Customs and Excise, who expect to receive *returns* from caterers usually every three months.

The operation of VAT

All caterers purchase commodities which, usually after some form of preparation, they resell to customers at a higher price. In order to understand the operation of the tax it is perhaps easiest to look at the operation of a public house first, and then consider a hotel or restaurant.

With the public house, the licensee purchases alcoholic and soft drinks for resale, usually from a brewery. When the brewery supplies him, it charges the licensee for all the beverages he has purchased, plus any deposits on the containers and then charges him value added tax on the total. The licensee pays the total to the brewery. As far as the Customs and Excise are concerned this payment of tax is called *input* tax. (Try not to be confused with the words — it may not seem logical to call something you have paid out *input* but as far as the Customs and Excise are concerned you, the licensee, have *imported* the goods on to your premises – hence *inputs*!)

The licensee now displays the goods he has purchased from the brewery in his bar and sells them at a higher price than he paid, and charges his customers VAT. This tax, that the licensee collects, is known as *output* tax (for the opposite reason to that given above).

At the end of the accounting period, usually every three months, the licensee should have collected more tax from his customers (*output tax*) than he has paid out to the brewery (*input tax*). He then simply subtracts the tax he has paid out for his supplies from the brewery from the tax he has collected from his customers and, having filled in the appropriate form, sends the balance to the Customs and Excise.

Example

(1) A typical VAT invoice will show the following:

	£
To goods supplied by Brewery Co	1000
VAT at 15%	150
TOTAL PRICE PAYABLE	£1150

(2)   At the end of the trading period, a typical (but simple) VAT return for our licensee may well look like this:

	£	£
Total outputs for the period (sales)	50 000	
VAT thereon (a)	7 500	7 500
Total inputs for period (purchases)	25 000	
VAT thereon (b)	3 750	3 750
Balance payable to customs and excise (a − b)		£3 750

The day-to-day dealing with VAT

It must be remembered that VAT is the *last* charge to be made to a customer. If we look at our licensee again, it is best explained if we look at how he formulates his price structure for his bar.

The licensee buys a bottle of Cognac from his brewery at a cost of £8.50 plus VAT £1.27½ p. The licensee proposes to sell 30 measures out of his bottle of Cognac, over the bar; and aims to make 50% Gross Profit (GP) on his outlay. He would, therefore, arrive at his selling price as follows:

> 1 bottle cognac £8.50 plus 50% GP £4.25 = Selling price £12.75
> £12.75 plus VAT at 15% £1.91 = Final selling price £14.66
> £14.66 divided by 30 (the number of tots) = Bar price 48.8 p

He would probably charge 49 p or even 50 p in practice, but on the assumption that he was able to charge 48.8 p per tot, then, once he had sold the whole bottle, he would have received, in his till, £14.66.

His *input* tax on the transaction was £1.27½ p and his *output* tax from the transaction was £1.91. He would therefore return to the Customs and Excise the balance or 63½ p. You will note that he has still made his 50% Gross Profit, his customers have paid him the additional £1.91 of which the licensee retained £1.27½ (being what he had already paid out) and the other 63½ p went to the Customs and Excise.

The same principle applies to all pricing structures within the catering industry, although all transactions are not as simple as the one shown above. The catering industry is required, by law, to display VAT-inclusive price lists for all its services, including food, drink and accommodation. It is usual, therefore, to record all takings (sales) as a VAT-inclusive value and at the end of the accounting period remove the VAT portion.

How to separate VAT out of inclusive sales

In order to understand the principle of mathematically sorting out the VAT portion from takings which include VAT, let us for the moment assume that the rate of VAT applied is 10%.

Now, if we take a figure of £1 and add VAT on to it at a rate of 10%, we arrive at an inclusive price of £1.10 p. If we now break the transaction down into units, we find the following:

$$£1.00 + 10\% = £1.10$$

$$or \quad (10 \times 10) + (1 \times 10) = (11 \times 10)$$

It follows, therefore, that if we divide the VAT-inclusive figure by 11, we will get an answer of 10, being the amount of VAT we added. Just to prove the principle with a more complicated figure, we could get:

$$£324.20 + 10\% \ VAT = £324.20 + £32.42$$

$$= £356.62 \ (VAT\text{-}inclusive)$$

The VAT can be separated out by dividing the inclusive figure by 11:

$$\frac{356.62}{11} = 32.42$$

We can in fact establish a rule — simply divide the VAT rate at any given time into 100 and add 1. The resultant figure is then used to divide all inclusive sales by to produce the VAT portion.

Thus:

if the VAT rate is 8% divide the inclusive sales by 13.5 to get VAT

if the VAT rate is 15% divide the inclusive sales by 7.66 to get VAT

if the VAT rate is 12½% divide the inclusive sales by 9 to get VAT

These figures are presented here as decimals. If you want to work in fractions, then the accurate method of calculating the VAT portion of inclusive figures is to multiply by the rate of VAT and divide by 100 + the VAT rate.

125

Thus:

when the VAT rate is 15%, multiply by $\dfrac{15}{115}$ or $\dfrac{3}{23}$ to get the VAT

when the VAT rate is $17\dfrac{1}{2}$%, multiply by $\dfrac{17\frac{1}{2}}{117\frac{1}{2}}$ or $\dfrac{7}{47}$ to get the VAT

when the VAT rate is 18%, multiply by $\dfrac{18}{118}$ or $\dfrac{9}{59}$ to get the VAT

when the VAT rate is 14%, multiply by $\dfrac{14}{114}$ or $\dfrac{7}{57}$ to get the VAT

Examples

(1)   Given the rate of VAT as 16%, find the tax portion of the following inclusive amounts: (a) £567.87; (b) £32.98; (c) 4386.65.

(a) $567.87 \times \dfrac{16}{116} = 567.87 \times \dfrac{4}{29}$ (b) $32.98 \times \dfrac{4}{29} = 4.55$

$= 78.33$

(c) $4386.65 \times \dfrac{4}{29} = 605.06$

(N.B. 16 will divide into 100 giving an answer of 6.25. Therefore, the same results will be produced by dividing the inclusive sum by 7.25.)

(2)   Using the same figures as in (1), but changing the rate to 13%, find the new tax portions.

(a) $567.87 \times \dfrac{13}{113} = 65.33$ (b) $32.98 \times \dfrac{13}{113} = 3.79$

(c) $4386.65 \times \dfrac{13}{113} = 504.66$

VAT on food in hotels and restaurants

So far the licensee has been receiving all the attention — the reason being that the majority of his *inputs* are of a taxable nature.

Many goods and services in our daily life are not subject to VAT at all (at present) and are therefore given an official rate of *zero.* The range is quite large, from such things as motorcyclists' crash-helmets to newspapers. However, the largest group, and one which concerns most caterers, is that of food. All food is zero-rated with the exception of pet foods, alcoholic drinks and such food products as crisps, ice-cream, chocolate and soft drinks (all the things most children like to eat!).

When the caterer buys in his meat, fish, poultry and so on, he does not pay any *input* tax. However, when he sells the food in his restaurant he must charge his customers VAT. The difference, therefore, between the licensee and the restaurateur is that the restaurateur has no *balance* to send to the Customs and Excise — he sends the lot!

After costing a dish to produce the required gross profit a restaurateur could produce the following as a typical bill for one of his customers:

	£
Cover charge	0.50
Meal charge	15.50
Subtotal	16.00
Service charge at 10%	1.60
Subtotal	17.60
VAT at 15%	2.64
Total payable	£20.24

Note that the VAT was the last thing to be added and it was, therefore, applied not only to the food but also the cover charge and the service charge.

Keeping records for VAT

Most hotels and caterers have some form of book-keeping which will show the day to day trading of the business. This may be in the form of a tabular ledger or some form of mechanical operation. Whatever its form, accurate records must be kept and it is as well to know, from day to day, just how much the business owes the Customs and Excise for VAT or vice versa.

A simple VAT summary, such as the one shown on the next page, can be filled in either weekly, daily or monthly according to when the business summarises its takings and expenses.

VALUE ADDED TAX SUMMARY

Inputs	VAT £	p	Taxable value £	p	Tax period:			
Goods for resale					Week No.			
Expenses								
TOTAL								
Opening balance					Zero rated goods		Exempt goods	
New balance					£	p	£	p

Outputs	VAT £	p	Standard rate goods £	p				
Takings	///	///						
VAT*					///	///	///	///
Net totals								
Opening balances								
New balances								
Input new balance					///	///	///	///
Net VAT balance			payable to		Customs and Excise			

*Obtained by dividing by 23 and multiplying by 3, if the rate of VAT is 15%

How to fill in the summary

(i) At the end of each trading period, to suit the individual business, enter the total spent (exclusive of VAT) on goods for resale (such as alcoholic beverages and food) under 'Taxable value' in the 'Inputs' section and the amount of VAT paid out under the heading VAT to the left.

(ii) Make similar entries on the expense line and take account of payments for equipment for the business and the usual overhead expenses like stationery, cleaning materials, etc.

(iii) Total these two figures and enter in the total line.

(iv) Now add the total produced from transaction (iii) to the opening balance to produce a new balance at the bottom of the Input Box. (This new balance becomes the opening balance for the next trading period.)

(v)   Record the gross takings (including VAT) on the line marked 'Takings' under the heading of 'Standard rate goods'.

(vi) Divide the gross takings by the appropriate number to separate the VAT portion out and record the answer once under the heading of VAT and once under the entry of gross takings, both on the line marked 'VAT'.

(vii) Subtract the VAT from the gross takings and write the answer on the line beneath marked 'Net totals'.

(viii) Add the net totals to the 'Opening balance' figures appearing beneath and record the answers on the line marked 'New balances'. (These figures are carried forward to the next accounting period as opening balances.)

(ix) Record the new balance for input VAT on the line provided and subtract one from the other. If the input balance figure is higher than the output balance figure the difference is owed to the business by the Customs and Excise and should be claimed. Usually the output balance is higher than the input balance, and the balance is payable to the Customs and Excise.

EXERCISE 47

1. If the VAT rate in force is 15% and an hotel had received £24 350 in sales from its restaurant (inclusive of VAT) what would be the VAT portion of the sales?

2. If the VAT rate were changed to 17½% what figure would you have to divide VAT-inclusive sales by in order to separate the VAT out?

3. Who is responsible for the administration of VAT on behalf of the Government, and when do they expect returns to be made to them?

4. If a bottle of wine is purchased from a wine merchant for £5.80, exclusive of VAT, and your restaurant expect to make 60% gross profit on sales, what must the selling price of the wine be, inclusive of VAT at 15%?

5. A nine-gallon cask of real ale is sold by a brewery to your hotel at a cost of £16.50, exclusive of VAT. Your hotel expects to make 50% gross profit on sales. What must the selling price be, per pint, inclusive of VAT at 12½%?

6. If the rate of VAT is 15% and the total tax-inclusive outputs for the period were £45 682 with the total tax-inclusive inputs £34 664, how much must either be sent or claimed from the Customs and Excise?

7. Complete the following restaurant bill for a customer:

	£ p
8 Luncheons, Table D'hôte at £6.45.	
Aperitifs.	3.80
Cover charge: 8 at 50 p	
2 × Bin 23 at £7.45	
Service charge at 12½%	
VAT at 15%	

8. Separate the VAT out of the following sales figures. The rate added was 16%.

(a) £67.45 (b) £7654.98 (c) £23 642.88 (d) £12.45

9. If the food cost for a banquet was £4.80 per person and 150 people are expected, how much would you quote for the event if your food cost percentage is 38%, service charge is 10% and the current rate of VAT is 15%?

10. You propose including Prawns in Cheese Sauce as a hot dish on your bar snack menu. At what price would you put it on if you expect to make 40% gross profit from sales and VAT is 15%? The food cost is £1.00.

11. If you bought one case of chocolate bars (48 in a case) and paid £6.72 for the case, inclusive of VAT at 15%, what would you charge for each bar if you expect to make 10% gross profit on sales after allowing for VAT?

12. A guest's bill comes to £56.80 inclusive of VAT. What would his bill be if you allowed him a discount of 10%? The current rate of VAT is 15%.

11
Business Viability

Introduction

In this chapter we will look at the viability of a business in the very simplest of terms and, even then, mainly from a clinical point of view. It is proposed to leave to the student and lecturer (or the purchaser and his bank manager!) any discussion they may wish to have about reasons other than financial ones for starting a business.

The vast majority of catering businesses today are of the small unit type; and with some 75000 public houses alone and probably somewhere in the region of 60000 restaurants we feel that the majority of students and prospective purchasers will be more concerned with this type of operation.

Why go into business?

There are many answers to this question: status; to get away from the boss who doesn't understand; to provide a roof over your head and thus cheap accommodation; or simply because it is a challenge and an interest or hobby. However, the best reason must be one of money. The cbject of business is to make a profit and, to a great extent, the way we keep score or measure the success of the business is to see how great that profit is.

One of the first questions which must be asked, before embarking on a business venture, is: will the business produce as much in profits for myself as I could earn if I worked for someone else? If the answer is yes, then go on to ask if it will, in addition, produce enough profit to give me a similar return on my capital invested as if I had invested in (say) a building society?

Let us consider the chef who has been working in a medium-sized restaurant and has been earning £6000 per year. He now has managed to save £50000 and would like to purchase his own restaurant.

If he invested his savings he could earn something like 15% per annum before tax, or £7500. If we add this to his salary of £6000 per annum we arrive at a figure of £13500 per annum, or £259.61 per week. Now, will the proposed restaurant produce

this sort of profit? Now you may well say: 'But what about his free accommodation and the capital appreciation?' Well, his 'free accommodation' is no longer 'free' if he is self-employed! The Inland Revenue will charge him a proportion of the expenses if he lives on the premises as if it were part of his income, and as for the capital appreciation — well, he would get that anyway if he bought his own house. Discussion could go on for some time on these sort of points so, perhaps, it would be better to leave it at that and start looking at business viability.

A profit and, if so, when?

Profit is the difference between the expenses (or cost of operation) and the income (or sales) the business will produce. In an ideal situation the business expenses would rise in proportion to the income and a profit would be made regardless of the income. Unfortunately, however, this is not so, certainly within the catering industry. Some of our catering expenses do rise and fall in proportion to our turnover, for example food or beverage costs. Caterers will buy more food as the demand for it rises and should the demand fall off then they will suspend purchases. The same follows for beverage purchases, with one distinct advantage — apart from beer purchases it does not go 'off'. In some cases it actually increases in value and may return much higher percentage profits than those anticipated. (1945 Vintage Port bought in 1973 for £4.50 per bottle was selling in 1980 for £45.00 a bottle.)

Most catering businesses, in addition to the expenses which rise and fall with the turnover (from now on we will call these *variable expenses*) have expenses which will remain constant whether or not any turnover is produced.

Overhead expenses

We have already discussed the expenses of food and drink. These are not however the only costs which a restaurateur or hotelier has to meet. He will have to pay for the electricity and pay for his staff. Such expenses are sometimes called *overhead expenses* or just *overheads.* We shall see that some of these are *fixed* and some are *variable.*

Fixed overheads

Fixed overheads, as we shall call them, are the ever-present ones like the rates. Every business must pay rates to the local council, and the local council are not too interested in how well your business is doing. Some catering businesses will, in fact, pay more in rates as their business improves. Public houses, for example, pay rates in proportion to their purchases from the brewery companies.

If capital has had to be borrowed in order to start the business, then whoever lent the money will require interest from you; and once again, they are not too concerned as to how well you succeed.

Most caterers employ some staff, even if only very basic key personnel. A restaurant, for example, will require at least one chef, one waiter, and one barman. These staff will expect to be paid each week or month and will not take too kindly to being told that they have not got any wage this week because the business was slack.

If we accept the above concepts, then it follows that at some time the profit produced from selling our products (food, drink and accommodation) will exactly meet all these fixed overheads; but as we sell more, then so our variable overheads rise. What must first be looked for is the point at which all the profit produced from our sales will exactly meet not only all the fixed overheads but also all the variable overheads. This point is logically known as the *break-even point* and may be expressed in terms of income or in terms of customers in a restaurant.

133

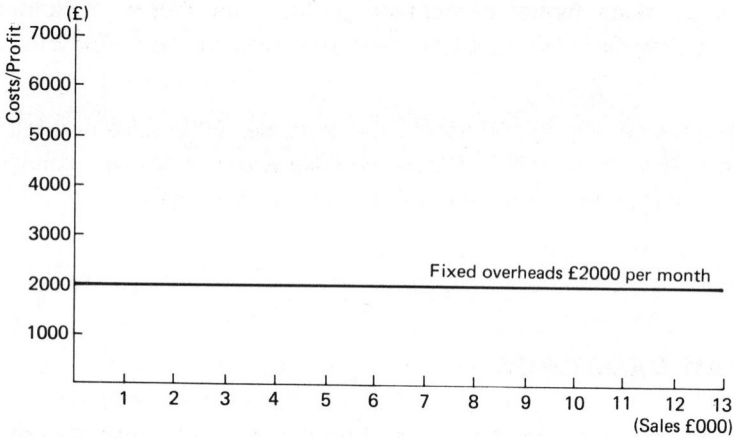

Perhaps the easiest way of representing fixed and variable overheads and expected profits is graphically.

The fixed overheads, known to the operator of the business, are added up, and, in the above example, are computed to monthly figures. The fixed overheads line is then drawn on the graph as a straight, horizontal line at the £2000 cost point.

In this example the business is a restaurant, with no licence, and the proprietor has decided to cost all his menu dishes so that he will receive 60% of his sales in the form of gross profit. In simple terms, his kitchen percentage is to be 40% or from every £1 he receives in income he has allowed himself 40 p to spend on food.

On the assumption that the caterer has costed his menu accurately, a line can be put on the above graph showing how much gross profit will be produced at all levels of turnover.

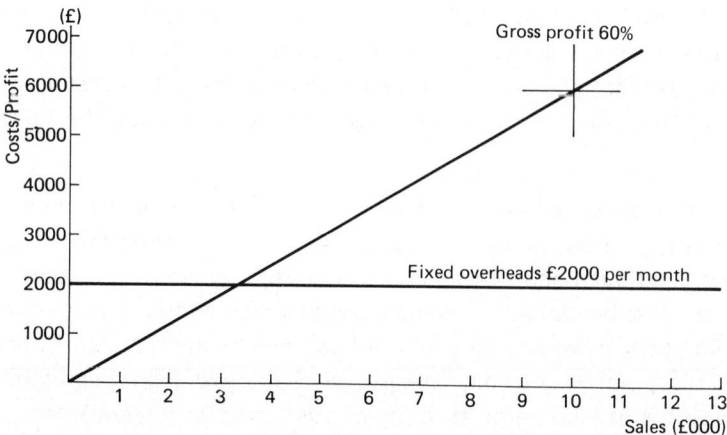

The gross profit line has been inserted so that at zero sales, zero profit is made and at £10 000 sales, £6000 gross profit will be made because 6000 is 60% of 10 000. It can be seen that the two lines cross at the point at which the sales are £3333.33. In other words, if the above restaurant only had the fixed overheads to worry about, it would need to take £3333.33 per month in order to meet all costs (60% of £3333.33 is £2000).

Variable overheads

As has already been mentioned, most businesses have variable overheads, such as the employment of more staff to cope with the increased business, more power to cook the food, increased laundry costs as more tablecloths are used, and perhaps more stationery, etc. Apart from the cost of staff, most of these variable costs are fairly small. It is even possible that some of the costs of running the business may go down as a result of increased business; for example, less heating may be required for the restaurant and perhaps some advertising could be cut out as well.

Variable overheads are usually given as a percentage of sales — say 10% or 20%. (This percentage can be estimated on the basis of past experience or by calculating the bills over a month. If you were thinking of buying a company you would estimate it from the past accounts.) Let us suppose that in our example they are 20%. We can now add these expenses to the graph above by drawing in a line XZ (see the diagram below) with a slope of 20%. To draw this line go £10 000 along the fixed overheads line to Y, then go 20% of £10 000 upwards to Z, i.e. £2000 upwards to where the cost value is £4000. Then draw a straight line through XZ. This line now gives the total overheads.

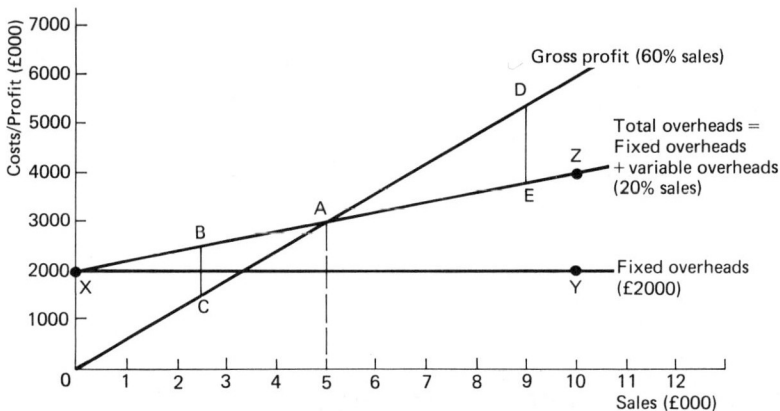

135

Loss or profit?

We have already learnt that the *gross profit* is the profit remaining when the food and drink have been paid for. When the overheads have been allowed for we are left with the *net profit.* In a sample equation

Net profit = Gross profit − Total overheads

The net profit will be zero when the gross profit and overheads are equal. Referring to the graph, we see that this happens at point A where the gross profit and total overheads lines cross, i.e. at £5000 sales. This is the break-even point. For sales above that value there will be a net profit, but for sales below £5000 there will be a net loss. When there is a loss we can write:

Net loss = Total overheads − Gross profit

We can summarise thus

Total overheads *more than* gross profit. Result: net loss
Total overheads *same as* gross profit. Result: break even
Total overheads *less than* gross profit. Result: net profit

If we want to work out the amount of net profit or loss we can measure the distance between the lines. Thus at £2500 sales the distance BC gives a net loss of £1000; at £9000 sales the distance DE gives a net profit of £1600.

These answers can also be worked out as follows:

(1) £2500 sales

Gross profit = 60% × £2500 = £1500

Total overheads = £2000 + (20% × £2500)

= £2000 + £500

= £2500

Net loss = Total overheads − Gross profit

= £2500 − £1500

= £1000

(2) £9000 sales

Gross profit = 60% × £9000 = £5400

Total overheads = £2000 + (20% × £9000)

= £2000 + £1800 = £3800

Net profit = Gross profit − Total overheads

$$= £5400 − £3800$$

$$= £1600$$

The number of customers required

So far the break-even point has been expressed in terms of a sales figure. After a business has been operating for a little while the average amount of money spent by a customer can be found simply by dividing the number of customers into the total sales figure (excluding VAT of course!). Once the average spending has been found then the break-even figure can be expressed in terms of the number of customers who must visit the establishment.

Taking the restaurant in the example above, and on the assumption that the average spending by customers is found to be £12 per person, per visit, then by dividing this figure into the break-even point of £5000, it can be seen that 417 customers are required to break even over a period of one month. Now if the restaurant is open for six evenings a week (closed for lunch service) then, on average, the restaurant will need to feed 18 customers per night. (If the above figures applied to an establishment you operated, you would probably find yourself with a certain feeling of elation when the 19th customer walks in!)

The above principles can also be applied when considering expansion of existing facilities — simply cost in any new expense such as the cost of borrowing the money, draw up the graph and read off to see whether it is going to be a profitable proposition.

Pricing dishes

At some time before any catering operation can start, decisions must be made about what to charge the customers for your dishes. It must be remembered that out of each portion of food sold (or each drink, or each night's accommodation) certain costs have to be met. In simple terms these are: the cost of the food (or drink, etc.), the cost of the staff, the overhead cost (being the contribution to heating, lighting, stationery, laundry, advertising, etc.) and, of course, the net profit.

If a dish sells for £1, for example, then the above figures might be represented as follows:

Food cost	40%	
Labour cost	25%	
Overheads	22%	} These three items, together, are gross profit.
Net profit	13%	

If the above percentages are related to a portion of food, with a value, then a clearer picture will be given:

Steak and Kidney Pie selling at £4.00 per portion

	£ p
Cost of food	1.60
Cost of labour	1.00
Overheads	0.88
Net profit	0.52
	£4.00

Generally speaking the cost of labour and the cost of overheads are fairly fixed, *but* the cost of food and net profit are not.

The purpose of running a restaurant or hotel is to make a *net profit.* No profit, no business! Therefore, if the selling price is fixed at £4.00 (because perhaps the demand will fall if the price is increased) then any alteration in any of the first three items will automatically alter the net profit.

For example:

Reduce the food cost to	£1.40	(Cheaper cut of meat?)
Cut the labour cost to	80 p	(How? Sack the chef?!)
Reduce overheads to	80 p	(Speed up the cooking? Turn the lights off? Cut the heating down?)

= *increased profit to £1.00*

If the new figures are applied to the previous example of break-even, it can be seen that the break-even point falls dramatically.

EXERCISE 48

You are considering the purchase of a tenancy of a public house. The cost of purchasing the liquor stock and the fixtures and fittings is £10 000 and you propose borrowing this sum from your bank, who are going to charge you an interest rate of 20% p.a. The rent, to the brewery is to be £2 000 per annum and the net rates are £1500 p.a. You anticipate employing a minimum number of staff and to start with will only have one cleaner at a cost of £30 per week. You estimate that other fixed expenses will be £20 per week and that your variable expenses will be 10% of sales. The current turnover of the business is (so the outgoing licensee informs you!) £500 per week (excluding tobacco) and the prices have been fixed to produce 40% gross profit from sales.

1. At what point will the business break even, in money terms, per week?

2. What is the value of the net profit if the sales remain at £500 per week?

3. You expect to be able to push up the sales to £750 per week. How much net profit can you expect to make?

4. You would like to earn £10 000 per annum for yourself, in the form of profits. What must your takings be in order to achieve this?

12
Nutrition

Introduction

In certain areas of the catering industry it is important to know the precise nutritional and energy content of a meal. In hospitals, for example, a dietitian supervises a patient's requirements and some people such as diabetics need special treatment for which specialised handbooks are available.

We shall see that working out the nutritional and energy content for each meal is a matter of knowing how much 'value' each gram of food has and knowing precisely how much the food weighs. Knowing the weight of the food is obviously very important as anyone on a diet would know — it is all very well saying 'that looks roughly 100 grams of bread', but you may have a shock if you put it on the scales. In previous chapters we have seen how weight is lost during cooking and this is important. Some vitamins (notably B and C) can also be lost and this too is important.

Units of energy

Heat and energy, which amount to the same thing, are measured in basic units of 1 calorie (abbreviated cal). This is defined by physicists as 'the amount of heat required to raise 1 gram of water by 1 °C at normal temperature and pressure'. In terms of people's daily requirements this is a very small amount of energy so we would more normally use the kilocalorie (abbreviated kcal), which is the same as 1000 calories. Sometimes this is simply called the Calorie or Cal (with a capital C instead of a small one!).

More recently nutritionists have started using the kilojoule (abbreviated kJ and equal to 1000 joules) and the megajoule (abbreviated MJ and equal to 1 million joules). There is a simple formula which relates the megajoule to the kilocalories:

1000 kcal = 4.2 MJ

This means that

$$1 \text{ kcal} = \frac{4.2}{1000} \text{ MJ}$$

and that

$$1 \text{ MJ} = \frac{1000}{4.2} \text{ kcal}$$

It is quite easy to convert from either unit to the other as these two examples show:

Examples

(1)   A man needs a daily intake of 3500 kcal. How many MJ is that?

$$\text{Since 1 kcal} = \frac{4.2}{1000} \text{ MJ}$$

$$3500 \text{ kcal} = \frac{3500 \times 4.2}{1000}$$

$$= 14.7 \text{ MJ}$$

(2)   I reckon the food I ate yesterday had a nutritional value of 16 MJ. What is that in kcal?

$$\text{Since 1 MJ} = \frac{1000}{4.2} \text{ kcal}$$

$$16 \text{ MJ} = \frac{16 \times 1000}{4.2}$$

$$= 3810 \text{ kcal}$$

Now try the following exercise.

EXERCISE 49

1.   Convert the requirements of the following individuals into MJ:
     (a) Jim 4000 kcal   (b) Joan 2500 kcal   (c) Jeremy 1500 kcal

2.   Convert the following nutritional values into kcal:
     (a) 12 MJ   (b) 18 MJ   (c) 20 MJ

Basal metabolic rate and energy requirement

If you sat down all day, did nothing and stopped thinking (perhaps you do sometimes!) your body would still need to use energy at a rate that is called the *basal metabolic rate* (or BMR) — simply in order to carry out its normal functions. This rate of energy usage will depend on age, sex and the body's surface area.

To work out the BMR you first of all use Chart 1 and then Chart 2 which is called a nomogram.

Age (yrs)	MALES		FEMALES	
	$Cal/m^2/hour$	$kJ/m^2/hour$	$Cal/m^2/hour$	$kJ/m^2/hour$
1	53	222	53	222
3	51.3	215	51.2	214
5	49.3	206	48.4	203
7	47.3	198	45.4	190
9	45.2	189	42.8	179
11	43.0	180	42.0	176
13	42.3	177	40.3	169
15	41.8	175	37.9	159
19	39.2	164	35.5	149
20	38.6	162	35.3	148
25	37.5	157	35.2	147
30	36.8	154	35.1	147
40	36.3	152	34.9	146
50	35.8	150	33.9	142
60	34.9	146	32.7	137
70	33.8	141	31.7	133
80	33.0	138	30.9	129

Chart 1. BMR tables in terms of the body's surface area

The way in which these charts are to be used should be clear from the following example.

Example
Find the daily energy requirement in MJ of a totally idle 19-year-old girl, 1.8 m tall, weighing 76 kg.

From Chart 1 we see that her BMR is 146 kJ/m²/hr. This means she uses 146 KJ every hour for every square metre of her body's surface area.

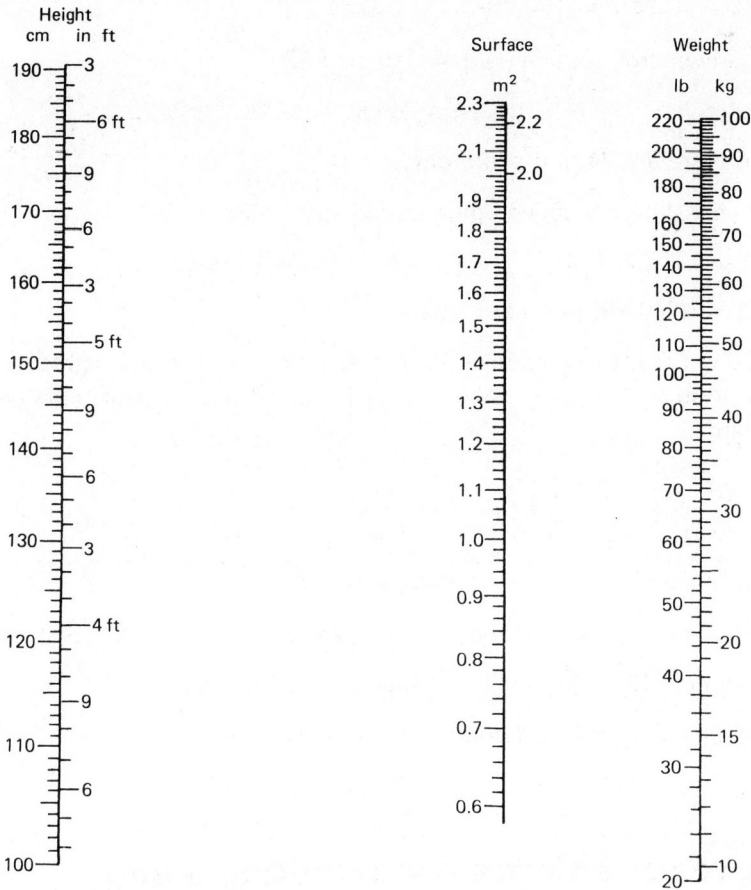

Chart 2. Nomogram for the estimation of body surface area

Now look at Chart 2 to see what her surface area is likely to be. Run a ruler from 76 kg across to 1.8 m. The ruler will cut across the middle diagram (see Chart 3) at a value of 1.96 m² which is therefore the girl's probable surface area.

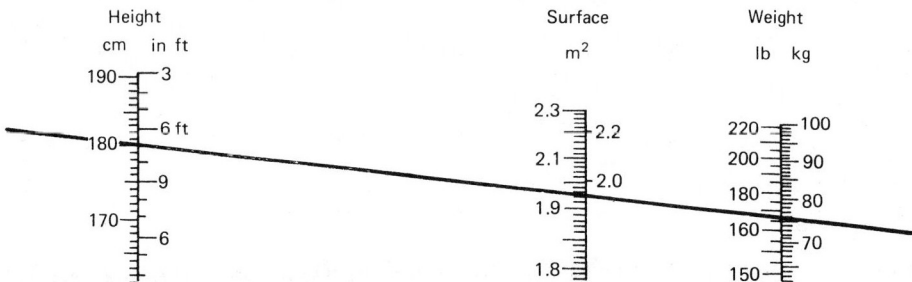

Chart 3. Example of use of nomogram

So

her hourly energy requirement = 149 × 1.92

= 256 kJ

Thus, since there are 24 hours in a day,

her daily basal metabolic energy requirement = 286 × 24

= 6884 kJ

Since 1 MJ = 1000 kJ, her requirement = 6.9 MJ

Note that Chart 2 also gives heights in feet and inches and weights in pounds (remember 14 lb = 1 stone). This may be helpful if not all your units are in the metric system.

EXERCISE 50

Find the basal metabolic energy requirement in MJ for:

1. Jim, who is 5, 110 cm tall and weighing 25 kg.

2. Stella, who is 13, 1.60 m tall and weighing 45 kg.

3. Dick, who is 25, 6′ 1″ tall and weighing 12 st 7 lb.

Energy requirements for everyday living

The normal daily energy requirements of an active person can be calculated by an analysis of that person's activity during 24 hours. This could, for example, be as shown in the following chart for Mr X.

Chart 4. A day in the life of Mr X

Each of these activities will require a certain amount of energy, and this will vary from activity to activity — you obviously need more energy dancing than you do when sleeping. Also the amount of energy for a particular activity will vary from individual to individual because people use up their energy at different rates. A heavy person will need more energy to dance than a light person because he has a bigger load to shift around, but sometimes people of the same weight will need different amounts of energy for the same activity. Why this is so is not completely understood. The table below shows some average figures of energy expenditure for a 25-year-old man weighing 65 kg:

Activity	RATE OF ENERGY (k cal/min)	EXPENDITURE (KJ/min)
Sitting	1.4	6
Washing, dressing	3.5	15
Walking briskly	5	21
Light work	2.5	10
Dancing	5.0	21
Squash	over 7.5	over 30

You can find figures for some other activities in the *Manual of Nutrition* published by HMSO.

We can now use some of these figures to work out the energy requirements for Mr X either in kcal or kJ. The table below shows how to work out Mr X's requirement in kcal:

Activity	Time (hours)	Time (min)	Activity metabolic rate (kcal/min)	Energy requirement (kcal)
Light work	8	480	2.5	1200
Sleep	8	480	1.1	528
Sitting	4 ½	270	1.4	378
Dancing	1 ½	90	5.0	450
Walking	1	60	5.0	300
Washing & Dressing	1	60	3.5	210
			TOTAL	3066

In the first row we see that work is done for 8 hours, 8 × 60 = 480 minutes and since the activity metabolic rate is 2.5 kcal/min the energy requirement is 480 × 2.5 = 1200 kcal. We work out the energy requirements for all the other activities and add up at the end.

EXERCISE 51
Draw up a table like the one above for Mr X and work out the daily energy requirement in kJ.

Energy intake

We have seen how to work out an individual's energy requirements. Now we must find a method to work out his or her energy intake. This is done by listing all foods and liquids taken in over 24 hours.

Most foods contain one or more of 4 basic nutrients: carbohydrates, fats, proteins and alcohol. 1 g of each of these will provide a certain amount of energy. Accepted values are shown in the table below.

Nutrient	Energy in kcal/g	Energy in kJ/g
Carbohydrates	3.75	16
Fats	9	37
Proteins	4	17
Alcohol	7	29

When the energy value of 100 grams of a stated food is known it is possible to calculate the energy content if you know how many grams of each nutrient the food contains.

Example
100 grams of fried chips contains: 1.1g protein, 2.6g fat, 10.6g carbohydrate. Therefore its energy value will be:

kcal		kJ	
1.1 × 4	4.4	1.1 × 17	18.7
2.6 × 99	23.4	2.6 × 37	96.2
10.6 × 3.75	39.75	10.6 × 16	169.6
Total	67.55	Total	284.5

The handiest source of information on the energy value of foods is the HMSO's *Manual of Nutrition* and it is recommended that you use this book in the exercises below.

EXERCISE 52

Find the energy value in kcal and kJ of 100 grams of:

1. Vanilla ice cream   **2.** Cornflakes   **3.** Cod fried in batter

4. Wholemeal bread   **5.** Roast chicken   **6.** Canned baked beans

How would you find the energy value of 50g or 10g of the same items?

Energy values for dishes

If a made-up dish is used its energy value is calculated by writing out a chart showing ingredients and amounts, and, then using the nutrition value tables to find the energy value of that amount of food.

Example
A fresh Fruit Salad giving 4 portions may be analysed as follows:

Food	Weight	kcal/100 g	To get kcal for correct weight	kcal/weight required
Orange	25 g	150	Divide by 4	8.75
Banana	30 g	76	Multiply by 0.3	22.8
Apple	60 g	46	Multiply by 0.6	27.6
Cherries	20 g	47	Multiply by 0.2	9.4
Pears	50 g	41	Divide by 2	20.5
Grapes	50 g	106	Divide by 2	53
Sugar	50 g	394	Divide by 2	193
Lemon juice	10 g	7	Divide by 10	0.7
			TOTAL	339.75

The number of kcal per person will be

$$\frac{339.75}{4} = 84.94$$

EXERCISE 53

A Fruit Salad for 4 people slightly different to the one above uses 30 g oranges (with energy value 150 kJ/100 g), 25 g banana (326 kJ/100 g), 50 g apple (197 kJ/100 g), 25 g cherries (199 kJ/100 g), 60 g pears (175 kJ/100 g), 50 g grapes (452 kJ/100 g), 50 g sugar (1680 kJ/100 g) and 10 g lemon juice (31 kJ/100 g). Work out the total energy value of the dish and the energy value for each portion.

EXERCISE 54

Use your own recipes and nutrition charts to find the energy intake of the following:

1. 50 g Apple Crumble
2. 1 portion Victoria Sandwich for 8 portions
3. 500 ml beer, 100 g bread, 10 butter, 100 g Cheddar cheese
4. 25 g bacon, 10 g tomato, 1 egg (50 g)
5. 1 portion Chicken in White Wine Sauce (Chicken chasseur)

Calculate your intake of energy on a typical working day. Would the above supply you with sufficient energy?

Nutrient intake other than energy intake

When trying to slim it is important to keep your energy intake below your energy output. (The greater this difference, the more likely the weight loss.) *However,* it should be remembered that the body needs a certain amount of all the nutrients and these must be supplied daily.

Chart 5 shows energy *and nutrient* requirements for a wide range of individuals. This can be used in conjunction with food value tables to plan suitable menus.

EXERCISE 55

1. (a) Find the Vitamin C content of 75 g orange.
    (b) Find the Iron content of 125 g of liver.
    (c) Find the Vitamin D content of 10 g butter.
    (d) Find the Thiamin content of 100 g Steak & Kidney Pie.
    (e) Find the Protein content of 50 g cornflakes.

2. Use Chart 5 and food value tables to plan a school meal menu for a 15-year-old boy. Make sure it has the legal requirement of protein in it.

Chart 5. Recommended daily intake in nutrients (Department of Health and Social Security, 1969)

Age ranges	Energy		Protein		Calcium	Iron	Vitamin A (retinol equivalent)	Thiamin	Riboflavin	Nicotinic acid equivalent	Vitamin C	Vitamin D
			Recom-mended	Minimum requirement								
years	MJ	kcal	g	g	mg	mg	μg	mg	mg	mg	mg	μg
Infants												
Under 1	3.3	800	20	15	600	6	450	0.3	0.4	5	15	10
Children												
1	5.0	1200	30	19	500	7	300	0.5	0.6	7	20	10
2	5.9	1400	35	21	500	7	300	0.6	0.7	8	20	10
3-4	5.7	1600	40	25	500	8	300	0.6	0.8	9	20	10
5-6	7.5	1800	45	28	500	8	300	0.7	0.9	10	20	2.5
7-8	8.8	2100	53	30	500	10	400	0.8	1.0	11	20	2.5
Males												
9-11	10.5	2500	63	36	700	13	575	1.0	1.2	14	25	2.5
12-14	11.7	2800	70	46	700	14	725	1.1	1.4	16	25	2.5
15-17	12.6	3000	75	50	600	15	750	1.2	1.7	19	30	2.5
18-34 sedentary	11.3	2700	68	45	500	10	750	1.1	1.7	18	30	2.5
18-34 moderately active	12.6	3000	75	45	500	10	750	1.2	1.7	18	30	2.5
18-34 very active	15.1	3600	90	45	500	10	750	1.4	1.7	18	30	2.5
35-64 sedentary	10.9	2600	65	43	500	10	750	1.0	1.7	18	30	2.5
35-64 moderately active	12.1	2900	73	43	500	10	750	1.2	1.7	18	30	2.5
35-64 very active	15.1	3600	90	43	500	10	750	1.4	1.7	18	30	2.5
65-74	9.8	2350	59	39	500	10	750	0.9	1.7	18	30	2.5
75 and over	8.8	2100	53	38	500	10	750	0.8	1.7	18	30	2.5
Females												
9-11	9.6	2300	58	35	700	13	575	0.9	1.2	13	25	2.5
12-14	9.6	2300	58	44	700	14	725	0.9	1.4	16	25	2.5
15-17	9.6	2300	58	40	600	15	750	0.9	1.4	16	30	2.5
18-54 most occupations	9.2	2200	55	38	500	12	750	0.9	1.3	15	30	2.5
18-54 very active	10.5	2500	63	38	500	12	750	1.0	1.3	15	30	2.5
55-74	8.6	2050	51	36	500	10	750	0.8	1.3	15	30	2.5
75 and over	8.0	1900	48	34	500	10	750	0.7	1.3	15	30	2.5
Pregnant, 2nd and 3rd trimesters	10.0	2400	60	44	1200	15	750	1.0	1.6	18	60	10
Lactating	11.3	2700	68	55	1200	15	1200	1.1	1.8	21	60	10

Crown copyright reproduced by permission

149

Wastage of nutrients

Nutritional tables often quote a figure for raw food. Allowances must then be made for parts of the food which cannot be eaten, e.g. the stone in a peach or the shell of an egg.

Example

Calculate the Vitamin A content of 200 g fresh whole apricots. Apricots contain 250 μg Vitamin A per 100 g and 13% waste. (NB μg is short for microgram and means one millionth of a gram. Although the weigh of vitamin you need is small, it is very important.)

$$200 \text{ g apricots contain } \frac{100 - 13}{100} \times 200 = 174 \text{ g edible matter}$$

$$174 \text{ g edible matter contains } \frac{\overset{87}{\cancel{174}}}{\underset{2}{\cancel{100}}} \times \overset{5}{\cancel{250}} \,\mu\text{g} = 435 \,\mu\text{g Vitamin A}$$

EXERCISE 56

Use nutrition tables and allow for wastage to work out:

1. Vitamin A content of 200 g peaches.

2. Protein content of 150 g raw chicken.

3. Iron content of 50 g egg.

4. Energy value of $\frac{1}{2}$ kg bananas, as purchased.

5. Thiamin content of 75 g bacon, as purchased.

Revision Exercises

1. Add the following:
    (a) 346.98
         567.23
         665.39

    (b) 454.77
         333.25
         267.66

    (c) 991.98
         767.14
         333.77

2. Multiply the following:
    (a) 56.89 ×
         34.56

    (b) 33.98 ×
         78.55

    (c) 98.78 ×
         12.97

3. Divide the following:
    (a) $12.5\overline{)364.88}$ (b) $45\overline{)678.77}$ (c) $56.89\overline{)12.78}$

4. What percentage is 23.4 of 70.2?

5. What percentage is 43.9 of 187.66?

6. What percentage is 789 of 1678.45?

7. What is $7\frac{1}{2}$% of £45.87?

8. What is 15% of £65.78?

9. What is 14% of £56.33?

10. What is 12% of £6.70?

11. What is 7% of £33.40?

12. If a restaurant bill *included* VAT at 15% and came to £24.67 how much would the VAT have been?

13. What four things make up the selling price of a meal in a restaurant?

14. A banquet has been planned in your hotel and the charge per person is to be £4.25. The number of persons attending will be 250. If the chef is working to a 40% food cost how much can he spend on food?

15. In order to make 60% gross profit on selling price how much must you sell a portion of food costing £1.33 for?

16. What formula would you use to convert °F to °C accurately?

17. How many pints are there in a litre?

18. How many pounds are there in a kilogram?

EXERCISE 58

1. A bottle of spirit costs £6.54. What is the value of $4\frac{7}{8}$ bottles?

2. A bottle of wine costs £3.46. What will the selling price be if the establishment wishes to make 45% gross profit and VAT is to be 15%?

3. A dish costs £5.37 to produce. The establishment wish to make 58% gross profit and VAT is $17\frac{1}{2}$%. What will the selling price be?

4. The sales from a restaurant are £34 678.56 for a period of one month. The cost of food sold for the same period is £14 839.32. What is the kitchen percentage for the period?

5. A hotel has 120 bedrooms and can accommodate 254 people. During one week the hotel let 684 rooms and accommodated 1078 people. What was the percentage room occupancy for the week and what was the percentage bed occupancy?

6. If 484 people ate in a restaurant over a period of seven days and between them spent £5488.56 inclusive of VAT at 15% what was the average spending per person, exclusive of VAT?

EXERCISE 59

1. What is the first principle, i.e. the most important principle, of food control?

2. A kitchen working on a food cost percentage of 40% will sell a portion of food costing £2.55 for how much?

3. Add a 15% service charge to the following restaurant bill: £24.88. What is the final total?

4. You are providing wine for a banquet of 250 people. The portion size is to be 5 fluid ounces and you are to allow $1\frac{1}{2}$ glasses per person. If a normal bottle contains 26 fl oz, how many bottles will you need to provide?

5. From your answer to Question 4 — if a bottle of wine retails at £3.50 per bottle, how much per cover will you have to charge for the wine?

6. A bottle of Scotch contains 32 measures (6-out size). If the cost price of one bottle is £4.25 how much must you charge per tot if you want to make a gross profit of 40% on sales?

7. A bottle of Tio Pepe sherry costs £2.06 and the usual size measure is 3-out per glass (or 16 measures per bottle). What will the selling price per measure be if you wish to make 50% profit on cost price plus VAT at 8%?

8. What is 9% of £30.00?

9. What will a Dover Sole cost if its weight is 400 g and the cost price is £2.40 per $\frac{1}{2}$ kg?

10. How would you find the gross profit for a restaurant at the end of the month? (Ignore beverages, i.e. consider food only.)

11. If you receive a code number of 104H, how much can you earn per week before you start paying tax?

12. Define the 'kitchen percentage'.

13. What would the effect be on the kitchen percentage if a restaurant cashier undercharged a customer on his bill?

14. What was the average customer spending if the food receipts were £2864 and the number of customers fed was 620?

15. If the opening stock of Scotch was $4\frac{3}{4}$ bottles and the purchases for the stock period were 8 bottles and the stock left at the end was $6\frac{7}{8}$, how much Scotch was consumed?

16. Multiply 46.87 by 35.90.

17. Express $\frac{1}{5}$th as a percentage.

18. If restaurant sales for one week were £1244 and the kitchen percentage is budgeted at 35% how much should the kitchen have spent on food?

19. Add 8% VAT to the following bill — £46.87.

20. Divide £687.89 by 78 customers.

EXERCISE 60

1. Convert the following to their accurate metric equivalents:
    (a) 4 lb stewing steak   (b) 1 lb butter
    (c) 6 oz plain flour   (d) 1 lb 8 oz onions
    (e) 8 oz kidney   (f) 1 oz seasoning

2. Convert the following to degrees Centigrade (accurately):

(a) 450 °F   (b) 82 °F   (c) 544 °F

3. Convert the following to degrees Fahrenheit (accurately):

(a) 25 °C   (b) 66 °C   (c) 70 °C

4. If your kitchen works on a 45% food cost, how much must you sell the following dishes for?

(a) Coq au vin (cost price 86 p)
(b) Chicken chasseur (cost price £1.02)
(c) Mushroom Soup (cost price 9 p)
(d) Steak and Kidney Pudding (cost price 65 p per portion).

5. If your kitchen is required to make 60% gross profit from sales, how much must you sell the following dishes for?

(a) Cheese and Tomato Omelette (cost price 27 p each)
(b) Fried Fillet of Plaice (cost price 69 p per portion)
(c) Fresh Fruit Salad and Fresh Cream (cost price 16 p per portion)
(d) Grilled Sirloin Steak (cost price £1.58 per portion).

6. If the sales from your restaurant for one week were £846, the kitchen food cost percentage was 40%, and labour and overheads were 28%, how much net profit did you make?

7. If the sales from your restaurant for one week were £1435 and the cost of the food you used in the kitchen was £642, what kitchen percentage did you in fact make?

EXERCISE 61

1. If the food takings from a banquet of 150 were £350 and your food cost for the banquet was £125: (a) what would the percentage gross profit be, and (b) how much did you spend on food per cover?

2. If a dish cost you £1.34 to produce and you had to make 45% gross profit, how much would you sell the dish for?

3. If you were fixing a selling price for a Table d'hôte menu, and during the costing you discovered that one dish cost very much more to produce than the others, what pricing action would you take?

4. When preparing soup for a banquet, approximately how much would you allow as a portion per cover?

5. How many glasses of wine would you expect to get out of one bottle?

6. Using a 3-out measure (usual for sherry measures) how many glasses would you expect to get out of a bottle containing $26\frac{1}{2}$ fluid ounces?

7. What is a hydrometer?

8. From Sunday morning until Saturday evening you are expected to serve 50 × 8 oz portion cups of coffee with milk per day.
   (a) How much coffee and milk will be required for a week?
   (b) What will it cost with coffee at £1.40 per lb and milk at £1.20 per gallon?
   (c) If you sell the coffee for 25 p a cup, what will be your gross profit percentage?

   (Assume 2 gallons of coffee can be made from 12 oz coffee and 1 gallon milk.)

EXERCISE 62

1. How would you arrive at your gross profit figure, in a restaurant, at the end of a month, after stocktaking?

2. Basically, what two items come out of gross profit?

3. The gross profit in a restaurant can be affected by a number of factors. Give five that you consider important.

4. If you were asked to show a 65% gross profit in a kitchen, how would you arrive at your selling price for each dish?

5. Considering metrication, what would you use as your basis for converting:
   (a) 1 kilo to lb oz?   (b) 1 litre to pints?

6. When converting oven temperature from degrees Centigrade to degrees Fahrenheit what approximate formula would you use?

7. A hotel adding $12\frac{1}{2}$% service charge and then 15% VAT on to a customers' bill of £12.40 would arrive at a hotel bill of what?

8. Who would make entries on a bin card?

9. Give two reasons for the issue of a Credit Note.

10. If you were offered discount by a supplier of meat, what would you check when the meat was delivered?

11. If the bone content of a leg of lamb is 25% and the weight loss during cooking is 15%, what usable weight of meat would you have left after cooking a 5 lb leg, and approximately how many 6 oz portions could you serve?

12. What method of portion control would you suggest for a dish such as Lancashire Hot Pot?

155

13. Give three methods of ensuring quality control of bottled beer in a bar.

14. Would you consider 260 °C too hot, too cool or just about right, for cooking a Victoria Sandwich Cake?

15. Define the kitchen percentage.

16. If the gross profit percentage is 60% what will the selling price be if the food cost is £3.60?

17. If the total sales for a month were £3546 and the cost of food sold was £1244, what was the kitchen percentage?

18. Explain the difference between the cost of food sold and the cost of food used.

19. Find 17% of £465.30.

20. Express 472 as a percentage of 9876.

EXERCISE 63

1. What is meant by purchasing tolerance?

2. What is a call-order dish?

3. Give four examples of food prices rising outside the control of the establishment.

4. A standard recipe should produce a standard yield. Give three reasons why this yield could differ from the budget.

5. Give one example of direct charges made to a kitchen.

6. Give three factors which would influence your choice of food supplier.

7. Give seven ways of making a menu more simple.

8. What do you consider to be the most important principle of food control?

9. A stocktaker, working in $\frac{1}{8}$ths produces the following count for proprietary gin: $3^2.5.1^6.5^1.9.3^4$. What is the total quantity?

10. If the cost price of rum is £5.75 per bottle, what is the value of 9^7 bottles?

11. The original price of beverages bought by a caterer was £346.50. He was allowed 5% cash discount. Calculate the amount paid by the caterer.

12. A hotel has 50 bedrooms. During one seven-day period it let 290. What was the hotel's room occupancy percentage for the period?

13. If £15 represents 30% of an amount, what would 50% be?

14. If the total takings for one week were £2348.45 *inclusive* of VAT (which had been added at the rate of 15%) what was the VAT portion of the takings?

15. A restaurant operates on a gross profit of 60% and has fixed costs of £12 000 p.a. It has been calculated that its variable expenses will be 25% of sales. Current sales are approximately £40 000 p.a. and the average customer spends £10 on a meal.

(a) What is the break-even point of the business in money terms?

(b) What is the current net profit?

(c) How many more customers would be needed per year to make a profit of £10 000?

16. If an item is bought for £1500 and it depreciates by 10% per annum, what is its book value in five years?

17. At the end of a month the restaurant takings were found to be £12 378.87 and after stocktaking in the kitchen it was found that the value of the opening stock was £876.98; the purchases for the month were £3897.40 and the value of the closing stock was £366.30.

(a) What was the value of the gross profit?

(b) What was the food cost percentage for the month?

18. An hotel bought an oven for £697 and is allowed a discount of £29.06 What is the percentage discount to the nearest $\frac{1}{2}$%?

19. The cost price of a side of beef, after deducting $12\frac{1}{2}$% discount, was £85. What was the original price?

20. By selling a bottle of Scotch for £8.50 a trader made a profit of 22% of his outlay. What would have been the percentage profit of outlay if he had sold the Scotch for £9.50?

EXERCISE 64

1. What will be the selling price if your food percentage is to be 43% and a portion costs:

(a) £1.35   (b) £2.24   (c) £1.86   (d) 85 p

2. If your target food percentage is 45% what is the gross profit from each of the following food bills and what is the total gross profit?

(a) £6.32   (b) £8.24   (c) £4.50   (d) £2.40

(e) £5.25   (f) £4.90

3.   What percentage of £82.00 are:

    (a) £24.00   (b) £32.36   (c) £44.20   (d) £52.30

    (e) £64.00?

4   Your share of the restaurant taking is $12\frac{1}{2}$%. What amounts will you receive from the following days' takings?

    (a) £84.00   (b) £120.00   (c) £150.00   (d) £75.25

5.   What are the following percentages of £50?

    (a) 14%   (b) 16%   (c) 6%   (d) 9%   (e) 23%   (f) 28%

6.   Accurately convert the following to degrees Fahrenheit:

    (a) 171 °C   (b) 177 °C   (c) 205 °C   (d) 260 °C

7.   Using a 6-out measure a bottle of spirit ($26\frac{2}{3}$ fl oz) will yield 32 measures. How many complete 6-out measures will you get out of:

    (a) 40 oz bottle   (b) a tregnum (equivalent to 3 bottles)

8.   Fill in the blanks:

    1 kilo = ... grams or .... ounces

    1 metre = ... millimetres or .... inches

    1 litre = ... millilitres or centilitres or ...... decilitres

9.   At the end of a month the restaurant takings were found to be £2437.87, and after stocktaking in the kitchen it was found that the value of the opening stock was £235.67, the food purchases for the month were £848.54, and the value of the closing food stock was £98.23.

    (a) What was the value of the gross profit?

    (b) What was the food percentage for the month?

Answers to Exercises

CHAPTER 1

Exercise 1

| 1. | 38 | 2. | 63 | 3. | 20 | 4. | 23 | 5. | 1762 | 6. | 8 |

Exercise 2

1.

£ p	£ p	£ p	£ p	£ p	£ p	£ p
26.32	280.46	926.33	24.52	167.84	4913.81	6339.28
41.22	32.87	41.26	145.11	222.45	231.90	714.81
113.56	22.64	11.83	29.00	12.68	1247.13	1436.84
33.23	334.19	112.76	431.98	1379.22	12.68	2304.06
214.33	670.16	1092.18	630.61	1782.19	6405.52	10794.99

2.

£ p	£ p	£ p	£ p	£ p	£ p
15.31	15.56	15.91	16.42	17.10	80.30
16.65	16.93	17.30	17.86	18.60	87.34
16.97	17.07	17.25	17.91	18.65	87.85
18.34	18.44	18.64	19.35	20.15	94.92
20.25	20.48	20.81	21.60	22.50	105.64
21.60	21.84	22.20	23.04	24.00	112.68
109.12	110.32	112.11	116.18	121.00	568.73

3.

£ p	£ p	£ p	£ p	£ p	£ p
19.81	20.03	20.59	21.36	22.25	104.04
20.65	21.00	21.22	22.03	22.94	107.84
20.65	21.00	21.22	22.03	22.94	107.84
22.00	22.37	22.61	23.46	24.44	114.88
20.50	20.50	20.50	20.50	20.50	102.50
21.00	21.00	21.00	21.00	21.00	105.00
24.00	24.00	24.00	24.00	24.00	120.00
25.00	25.00	25.00	25.00	25.00	125.00
35.00	35.00	35.00	35.00	35.00	175.00
208.61	209.90	211.14	214.38	218.07	1062.10

4.

£ p	£ p	£ p	£ p	£ p	£ p
26.26	26.55	27.29	28.32	29.50	137.92
39.40	39.40	39.40	39.40	39.40	197.00
44.75	44.75	44.75	44.75	44.75	223.75
21.00	21.00	21.00	21.00	21.00	105.00
22.50	22.50	22.50	22.50	22.50	112.50
31.00	31.00	31.00	31.00	31.00	155.00
32.00	32.00	32.00	32.00	32.00	160.00
35.00	35.00	35.00	35.00	35.00	175.00
49.00	49.00	49.00	49.00	49.00	245.00
39.00	39.00	39.00	39.00	39.00	195.00
27.50	27.50	27.50	27.50	27.50	137.50
28.00	28.00	28.00	28.00	28.00	140.00
37.75	37.75	37.75	37.75	37.75	188.75
433.16	433.45	434.19	435.22	436.40	2172.42

Exercise 3

1. £12.81   **2.** £60.71   **3.** £83.95   **4.** £625.81   **5.** £159.57   **6.** £711.97

Exercise 4

1. (a) 7270956   (b) 10741500   (c) 4408533   (d) 367505

2. (a) 99654   (b) 47223   (c) 68731.2

Exercise 5

1. (a) 9   (b) 25   (c) 11   (d) 13 remainder 2, i.e. $13\frac{1}{6}$ (e) 28

2. (a) 918.64   (b) 669.55   (c) 314.37   (d) 635.11   (e) 7.66
   (f) 2.19   (g) 8.29   (h) 83.54   (i) 214.59   (j) 475400

3. (a) 39.67   (b) 481.57   (c) 2853   (d) 242.69   (e) 1.10
   (f) 185.69   (g) 0.88   (h) 0.96   (i) 0.67   (j) 0.75

Exercise 6

1. (a) 3 (b) 5   **2.** (a) 2 (b) 6   **3.** (a) 0 (b) 4   **4.** (a) 3 (b) 5

5. (a) 4 (b) 3   **6.** (a) 3 (b) 4   **7.** (a) 3 (b) 5   **8.** (a) 0 (b) 2

Exercise 7

1.   (a) 57.498   (b) 43.596   (c) 558.48

2.   (a) 27.5   (b) 9.138   (c) 12.204

Exercise 8

1. 746.581   **2.** 1058.499   **3.** 1380.13

Exercise 9

1.   (a) 64.852   (b) 3.4   (c) 1289.565

2.   (a) 275   (b) 144000   (c) 129000

Exercise 10

1. 8, 17, 8, 11 2. 5, 13, 4, 12 3. (b), (i)

4. (d), (e), (g), (h), (i), (j) 5. (a), (c) 6. (f)

7. 2

8. (a) $3\frac{1}{9}$ (b) $5\frac{1}{2}$ (c) $4\frac{1}{5}$ (d) $2\frac{12}{13}$ (e) $3\frac{1}{9}$

9. (a) $\frac{11}{5}$ (b) $\frac{87}{12}$ (c) $\frac{11}{8}$ (d) $\frac{86}{15}$ (e) $\frac{39}{18}$

Exercise 11

1. $\frac{9}{15}$ 2. $\frac{9}{30}$ 3. $\frac{2}{3}$ 4. $3\frac{1}{3}$ 5. $2\frac{1}{4}$

6. $\frac{4}{7}$ 7. $\frac{1}{3}$ 8. $\frac{3}{5}$ 9. $\frac{2}{3}$ 10. $\frac{11}{12}$

Exercise 12

1. $4\frac{5}{12}$ 2. $2\frac{19}{40}$ 3. $4\frac{5}{12}$ 4. $5\frac{47}{52}$ 5. $1\frac{71}{168}$

Exercise 13

1. $9\frac{9}{16}$ 2. $6\frac{17}{18}$ 3. 7 4. $337\frac{13}{15}$

5. 3 6. $16\frac{1}{13}$ 7. $34\frac{1}{6}$ 8. $\frac{5}{36}$

Exercise 14

1. $3\frac{1}{3}$ 2. $2\frac{2}{5}$ 3. $\frac{1}{2}$ 4. $\frac{1}{9}$ 5. $12\frac{1}{2}$ 6. $\frac{3}{20}$ 7. $13\frac{1}{3}$ 8. $7\frac{1}{2}$

Exercise 15

1. $8\frac{7}{10}$ 2. $\frac{1}{10}$ 3. $\frac{1}{3}$

Exercise 16

1. 9.49 2. 13.98 3. 173 4. 7.37 5. 1.92 6. 18.4 7. 582.45 8. 60 p

Exercise 17

1. 33.09 2. 26.38

Exercise 18

1. £25.68 2. £14.02 3. 10.64% 4. 75.9% 5. 82.2%

6. 4 students 7. £7.92 8. £43.52 9. 120% 10. £3,773.50

Exercise 19

1. 1% 2. 37½% 3. 275% 4. 12½%
5. 5% 6. 33⅓% 7. 16⅔% 8. 37½%

161

Exercise 20

1. (a) $\dfrac{3}{4}$ (b) $\dfrac{9}{50}$ (c) $\dfrac{4}{10}$ (d) $\dfrac{1}{16}$ (e) $\dfrac{3}{5}$ (f) $\dfrac{2}{3}$ (g) $\dfrac{1}{8}$ (h) $\dfrac{3}{8}$

2. (a) 0.6   (b) 0.11   (c) 0.8   (d) 0.01   (e) 0.07
   (f) 0.3   (g) 0.78   (h) 0.5   (i) 0.1   (j) 0.85

3.

Vulgar fraction	Decimal fraction	Percentage
$\dfrac{2}{3}$	0.67	$66\dfrac{2}{3} = 66.67$
$\dfrac{43}{100}$	0.43	43
$\dfrac{3}{5}$	0.60	60
$\dfrac{1}{20}$	0.05	5
$\dfrac{3}{4}$	0.75	75
$\dfrac{1}{8}$	0.125	$12\dfrac{1}{2} = 12.5$
$\dfrac{21}{25}$	0.84	84
$\dfrac{3}{8}$	0.375	$37\dfrac{1}{2} = 37.5$

Exercise 21

1. £38.42   **2.** £27.05   **3.** £37   **4.** £17.25   **5.** £146.32   **6.** £2.02

Exercise 22

1. £8.91   **2.** £7.03½   **3.** £86.43   **4.** £1.23   **5.** £16.84   **6.** £27.51

CHAPTER 3

Exercise 23

1. 1 ton   **2.** Pail   **3.** Normal   **4.** 225 g
5. 35 °C   **6.** 16   **7.** 4   **8.** 1 quart
9. $4\dfrac{3}{4}$ **10.** 90 cm   **11.** 10 miles   **12.** No
13. 1 lb   **14.** 5 ml   **15.** 45 litre   **16.** 173 grams for 23 p
17. 45 cc   **18.** 45 cm   **19.** 70 cl   **20.** 500

Exercise 25

1. (a) 225 °C   (b) 400 °F   (c) 175 °C   (d) 300 °F
2. (a) (i) 90 °F   (ii) 86 °F   (b) (i) 38 °F   (ii) 41 °F
   (c) (i) 230 °F   (ii) 212 °F
   (d) (i) 1 °C   (ii) 0 °C   (e) (i) 142 °F   (ii) 133 °F
   (f) (i) 210 °F   (ii) 232 °F
   (g) (i) −50 °F   (ii) −40°F   (h) (i) −16 °C   (ii) −19 °C

Exercise 29

1. (a) £18.90 (b) 25 p (c) £6.56 (d) £7.59
2. (a) 85 p (b) 47 p (c) £2.56 (d) £2.08
3. (a) £6.44 (b) £589.05 (c) £7.20 (d) 84 p

Exercise 30

1. (a) 12.10 (b) 6.35 (c) 19.11 (d) 21.27
   (e) 22.30 (f) 21.30 (g) 2.16 (h) 00.10
2. (a) 7.09 p.m. (b) 12.55 p.m. (c) 8.30 p.m. (d) 10.12 p.m.
   (c) 8.05 p.m. (f) 6.00 a.m. (g) 5.05 p.m. (h) 12.15 a.m.

CHAPTER 4

Exercise 31

1. $33\frac{1}{3}\%$ 2. 50% 3. 40%

Exercise 32

1. (a) £6.88 (b) £6.11 (c) £9.17 (d) £5.50
2. (a) 38 p (b) 33 p (c) 50 p (d) 30 p
3. (a) 55 p (b) 49 p (c) 73 p (d) 44 p
4. (a) 60 p (b) 53 p (c) 80 p (d) 48 p

Exercise 33

1. (a) 35% (b) 70% (c) 72% (d) 62% (e) 60%
2. (a) 32% (b) 30% (c) 42% (d) 55% (e) 33⅓%

Exercise 34

1. 80% 2. 66⅔% 3. 44.4%

Exercise 35

1. (a) 95 p (b) 9½ p
2. (a) £2.55 (b) 6 p (c) (i) 6 p (ii) 6 p (iii) 7 p

CHAPTER 6

Exercise 43

2. £15.68
3. (a) £7854 (b) £7369 (c) £6787 (d) 52.05% (e) £1705.80 short fall

CHAPTER 7

Exercise 44

1. 37 p per glass

2. 42 p per pint

3. Incorrect change may be revealed by:
    (a) Customers complaining
    (b) Presence of price lists (now a legal requirement)
    (c) Surplus or deficiency in the till at the end of the day
    (d) Stocktaking
    (e) Other staff noticing.
    Effect on stocktaking could be:
    (a) Surplus (consistent with over-charging)
    (b) Deficiency (consistent with under-charging)
    (c) No effect (compensating short change with giving too much change).

4. 5 gallons will produce 800 fl oz or 30 bottles
    30 bottles will give 480×3-out tots or $240 \times 1\frac{1}{2}$ -out tots.
    Selling price per 3-out tot will be 14 p.
    Selling price per $1\frac{1}{2}$ -out tot will be 28 p.

5. Selling price per bottle will be 44 p.

6.

Cost	Product	Stock remaining	Total	Valuation £	p
2.20	Martini	$2^4.3^1.6.$	11^5	25	58
3.40	Cinzano	$1^2.5^3.4.$	10^5	36	13
4.75	Scotch	$12.3^1.2^5.1^1$	18^7	89	66
6.56	Cognac	$8^1.4.2.1^4.$	15^3	102	50
8.86	V.S.O.P.	$5.2.7.$	7^7	69	77
17.20	Keg Beer	40.6.7.	53	91	16
3.20	Pale Ale	$4^3.6^4.14^8.$	25^3	80	80
				495	60

(a) £1327.00
(b) £1049.30
(c) Actual gross profit $=$ £1049.30

Therefore   Gross profit percentage $= \dfrac{£1049.30}{£2376.30} \times 100$
$= 44.16\%$

(d) Cost of consumption $=$ £1327.00
So for 45% gross profit percentage we need 55% bar percentage

Therefore   sales should be $\dfrac{£1327.00}{0.55} = £2412.73$

But sales were £2376.30
Therefore   deficiency $=$ £2412.73 $-$ £2376.30
$=$ £36.43

CHAPTER 8

Exercise 45

1. Profit rises by £73.65   **2.** 0.6%   **3.** 40.8%

CHAPTER 9

Exercise 46

1. The rate per hour is £1.50. At time and a quarter it is £1.87½. At time and threequarters it is £2.62½. At double time it is £3.00. Therefore for 58 hours he would be paid the following:

	£
Basic Pay	60.00
4 at 1¼	7.50
4 at 1¾	10.50
10 at £3	30.00
Gross pay for the week	£108.00

2. The code number will be made up by adding all the allowances and removing the last figure. Therefore, in this case, the result would be:

$$985 + 28 + 645 + 54 = 1712$$

Therefore the Code Number will be 171.

3. The tax payable on the first £750 will be £187.50.
The remaining £2450 will be taxed at 30% or £735.00.
Therefore the tax liability over the year would be £922.50.

4. £7500 less personal allowances of £2450 will leave a taxable income of £5050. The first £750 will be taxed at 25% (£187.50) and the remaining £4300 will be taxed at 30% (£1290). Therefore the tax liability of this case will be £1477.50.

CHAPTER 10

Exercise 47

1. £3176.09   **2.** 6.714, but more accurately multiply by $\frac{7}{47}$.

3. The Customs and Excise; every three months.   **4.** £16.67½

5. 51.6 p, or 52 p commercially.   **6.** £1437.13 payable to Customs and Excise.

7. Food and service total:
£74.30 + Service charge £9.29 = £83.59 + VAT £12.54 = Grand total £96.13.

8. (a) £9.30   (b) £1055.86   (c) £3261.09   (d) £1.72

9. Costing per person produces a selling price of £15.98 or £2397.00 for the event.
Costing as a complete event produces a total inclusive bill of £2396.84.

10. £1.92   **11.** 15½ p or 16 p   **12.** £51.12

CHAPTER 11

Exercise 48

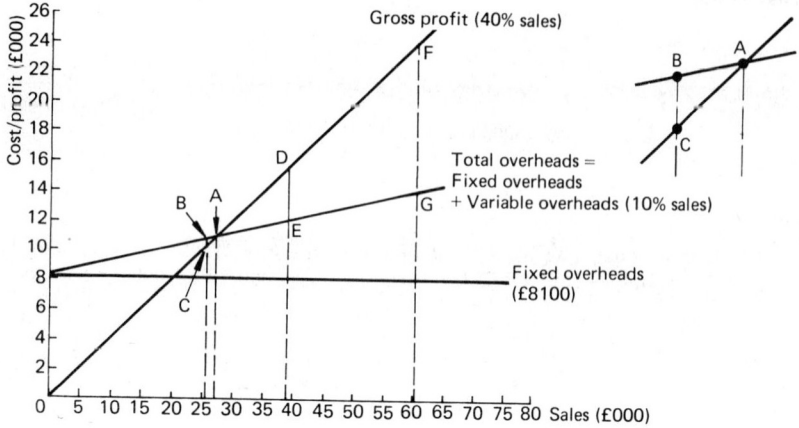

Graphically

1. Break-even point = £27000 pa or £519 per week (point A).

2. There is no profit. Net loss = BC = £300 (p.a.).

3. Net profit = DE = £3600.

4. £10000 net profit is where FG = £10000, i.e. at just over £60 000 sales (it is difficult to be more accurate than this using a graph).

Alternative methods using formulae:

1. At break-even

    Gross profit = Total overheads
    40% sales = £8100 + 10% sales
    ∴ 30% sales = £8100

    or sales $= \dfrac{£8100}{30} \times 100 = 27000$ p.a.

2. Net loss = Total overheads − Gross profit
    = (£8100 + 10% × £26000) − 40% × £26000
    = £8100 − 30% × £26000
    = £8100 − £7800
    = £300 p.a.

3. Net profit = Gross profit − Total overheads
    = 40% × £39000 − [£8100 + (10% × £39000)]
    = 30% × £39000 − £8100
    = £11700 − £8100
    = £3600

4. Net profit = Gross profit − Total overheads
    £10000 = 40% × sales − [£8100 + (10% × sales)]
    £10000 = 30% sales − £8100
    £18000 = 30% sales

    Sales $= \dfrac{£18100 \times 100}{30} = £60333.33$ p.a.

    = £1160.26 per week

CHAPTER 12

Exercise 49

1. (a) Jim 16.8 MJ   (b) Joan 10.5 MJ   (c) Jeremy 6.3 MJ

2. (a) 2857 kcal   (b) 4286 kcal   (c) 4762 kcal

Exercise 50

1. 4.20 MJ   2. 5.11 MJ   3. 7.45 MJ

Exercise 51

Activity	Time (hours)	Time (mins)	Activity metabolic rate (kJ/min)	Energy requirement (kJ/min)
Work	8	480	10	4800
Sleep	8	480	5	2400
Sitting	4½	270	6	1620
Dancing	1½	90	21	1890
Walking	1	60	22	1320
Washing & Dressing	1	60	15	900
			TOTAL	12930

Exercise 52

1. 166 kcal, 698 kJ   2. 368 kcal, 1567 kJ   3. 199 kcal, 834 kJ

4. 216 kcal, 918 kJ   5. 142 kcal, 599 kJ   6. 64 kcal, 270 kJ

(Divide by 2 or 10)

Exercise 53

Food	Amount	kJ/100 g	To get kJ for correct weight	kJ/weight required
Orange	30 g	150	Multiply by 0.3	45
Banana	25 g	326	Divide by 4	81.5
Apple	50 g	197	Divide by 2	98.5
Cherries	20 g	199	Multiply by 0.2	39.8
Pears	60 g	175	Multiply by 0.6	105
Grapes	50 g	452	Divide by 2	226
Sugar	50 g	1980	Divide by 2	840
Lemon juice	10 g	31	Divide by 10	3.1
			TOTAL	1438.9

Energy value per portion $= \dfrac{1438.9}{4} = 359.7$ kJ

Exercise 54
(Answers may vary slightly depending on recipes chosen)

1. 140.5 kcal, 588.5 kJ

2. 186 kcal, 777 kJ.

3. Beer: 155 kcal, 645 kJ.   Bread: 66 kcal, 281 kJ.
    Butter: 21 kcal, 86.2 kJ.   Cheese: 357 kcal, 1489 kJ.

4. Bacon: 112 kcal, 485 kJ.   Tomato: 1.4 kcal, 6 kJ.
    Egg: 73 kcal, 306 kJ.

5. 266 kcal, 1112 kJ. Total: 1377.9 kcal, 5775.7 kJ (or 5.78 MJ). Not enough energy!

Exercise 55
(Answers using *Manual of Nutrition*)

1. (a) 37.5 mg   (b) 14.2 mg   (c) 0.076 μg   (d) 0.14 mg   (e) 4.3 g

Exercise 56
(Answers using *Manual of Nutrition*)

1. 144.4 μg   2. 17.6 g   3. 0.88 mg   4. 228 kcal   5. 0.24 mg

REVISION EXERCISES

Exercise 57

1. (a) 1579.60   (b) 1055.68   (c) 2092.89

2. (a) 1966.1184   (b) 2669.129   (c) 1281.1766

3. (a) 29.1904   (b) 15.083 778   (c) 0.224 644

4. 33 1/3 %   5.   23.4%   6.   47%   7. £3.44   8.   £9.87

9.   £7.89   10. 80 p   11. £2.34   12. £3.21

13. Food, labour, overheads, profit   14. £425   15. £3.33

16. $^{\circ}C = (^{\circ}F - 32) \times \dfrac{5}{9}$ 17. 1.76 pints   18. 2.2 lb

Exercise 58

1. £31.88   2. £7.23   3. £15.02

4. 42.79   5. Room occupancy = 81.43   6. £9.86
                            Bed occupancy = 60.63

Exercise 59

1. Stock security   2. £6.37½   3. £28.61   4. 73   5. £1.02

6.   22 p   7. 21 p   8. £2.70   9. £1.92

10. Opening stock + Purchases − Closing stock = Gross profit

11. £20 (liable to change on Budget)

12. The amount of money the kitchen can spend on food

13. It would rise.

14. £4.62   15. $5\dfrac{7}{8}$ 16. 1,682.633

17. 20%   18. £435.40   19. £50.62

20. £8.82

Exercise 60

1. (a) 1814.4 g (or 1.81 kg)   (b) 453.6 g   (c) 170.1 g
   (d) 680.4 g   (e) 226.8 g   (f) 28.4 g

2. (a) 232 °C   (b) 27.7 °C   (c) 284.4 °C

3. (a) 77 °F   (b) 150.8 °F   (c) 158 °F

4. (a) £1.91   (b) £2.27   (c) 20 p   (d) £1.44

5. (a) 67½ p   (b) £1.72½ p   (c) 40 p   (d) £3.95

6. £270.72   7. 44.7%

Exercise 61

1. (a) 64.3%   (b) 83 p

2. £2.44

3. Either omit the dish or place an additional charge on that dish, i.e. guests ordering that dish pay the menu price plus the additional charge.

4. 3 to ½ litre or 150 ml.

5. 6 from 70 cl.

6. 15.996 measures = 16 in practice

7. An instrument for measuring the density of a liquid.
   (a) 17.5 gallons
   (b) £9.19 coffee, £10.50 milk
   (c) £64.75 = 77.5% gross profit

Exercise 62

1. Sales − (Opening stock + Purchases − Closing stock).   2. Overheads and net profit.

3. Increases in food prices; poor portion control; excessive wastage; staff stealing; deterioration of food through bad storage; incorrect costing; poor accounting; poor cooking resulting in customer complaints.

4. $\frac{\text{Food cost}}{35} \times 100$ = Selling price.   5. 2.2 lb = 1 kg; 1.75 pints = 1 litre

6. °F = °C × 2   7. £16.04

8. The person in charge of the stores or cellar.

9. Return of containers for which a deposit has been charged; the return of goods to the supplier; the non-arrival of goods which have been invoiced.

10. The quality, the quantity and the price charged.

11. 3 lb 3 oz; 8 portions.

12. The most accurate would be individual dishes.

13. Accurate stock rotation; correct temperature control; cleanliness.

14. 260 °C is approximately 520 °F and, therefore, too hot.

15. The kitchen percentage is the value of food sold by a kitchen expressed as a percentage of sales.

16. £9.00   17. 35.08%

18. The cost of food used may well include items of food which were not, in fact, actually sold. These would be for such items as fruit and cream for the bar, food given away to customers who have complained, and management entertaining. The cost of food sold should be a net item and only include that food which was, in fact, actually sold.

19. £79.10   20. 4.8%

Exercise 63

1. The amount by which incoming supplies may vary from what was ordered.

2. A dish which is not cooked until it is ordered.

3. Natural shortage because of weather, poor harvests etc.; transport difficulties creating shortages; increases in consumer demand.

4. Poor cooking (excessive cooking reducing the yield, undercooking either making the food unacceptable or altering the yield); poor carving; poor portion control.

5. Food sent/issued directly to the kitchen such as meat, fish, vegetables and dairy products.

6. Reliability, convenience for supply, price.

7. Reducing the number of dishes; restricting the dishes to the call order type; including only dishes with limited ingredients; using only the unit type of foods such as chops, pre-portioned steaks; using convenience foods — particularly the boil-in-the-bag variety; leaving the menu in operation for a long period of time; using only foods which require a short cooking time.

8. Stock security.   9. 28^3 i.e. 28⅜   10. £56.78   11. £329.18

12. 82.86%   13. £25   14. £306.32

15. (a) £34285.71   (b) £2000.00
    (c) Sales required to produce £10000 net profit would be £62857.14. Therefore an increase in sales of £22 857 is required or, at £10 per meal per person, 2286 customers per year.

16. £885.74   17. (a) £7970.79 (b) 35.61%   18. 4%   19. £97.14   20. 36.35%

Exercise 64

1. (a) £3.14   (b) £5.21   (c) £4.33   (d) £1.98

2. (a) £3.48   (b) £4.53   (c) £2.48   (d) £1.32
   (e) £2.89   (f) £2.69   Total £17.39

3. (a) 29.27%   (b) 39.46%   (c) 53.9%   (d) 63.78%
   (e) 78.05%

4. (a) £10.50   (b) £15.00   (c) £18.75   (d) £9.41

5. (a) £7   (b) £8   (c) £3   (d) £4.50
   (e) £11.50   (f) £14

6. (a) 339.8 °F   (b) 350.6 °F   (c) 401 °F   (d) 500 °F

7. (a) 48   (b) 95.99

8. 1 kilo = 1000 grams or 35 ounces
   1 metre = 1000 millilitres or 39 inches
   1 litre = 1000 millilitres or 100 centilitres or 10 decilitres

9. (a) £1451.89   (b) 40.4%